VANISHING
ANN
ARBOR

PATTI F. SMITH
AND BRITAIN WOODMAN

THE
History
PRESS

Published by The History Press
Charleston, SC
www.historypress.com

(Front cover) With permission of Barcroft Studios.

(Back cover, top) 1910 Washtenaw Avenue. *From the Bentley Historical Collection postcard collection.*

First published 2019

Manufactured in the United States

ISBN 9781467140256

Library of Congress Control Number: 2019935341

Thanks to my husband, Ken Anderson, for all of his support. I love you very much! Thanks to the people of our great city for taking me in, making a place for me and supporting me in my various crazy endeavors. I also love you very much.

—Patti Smith

Thank you to my spouse, Abbey, for her support in all of my writing projects, and to each of our families, especially the family members that encouraged us each to move to Ann Arbor and eventually meet each other. Special dedication to the people who started (and ended) dreams in Ann Arbor, and to my friends who experienced many of these lost institutions with me in their day. I wouldn't be trying to preserve their memory if it weren't for you.

—Britain Woodman

CONTENTS

ACKNOWLEDGEMENTS

A million thanks to Sarah Smalheer for her ace copyediting help; the wonderful gang at Ann Arbor District Library archives; the awesome folks at Bentley Historical Library; the lively and never boring Ann Arbor Townies Facebook page; Sam Bagenstos, Susan Wyman and Jane Berliss-Vincent for bailing us out of a jam; and our families and friends who make this such a great place to live!

INTRODUCTION

Ann Arbor is a special place—it affects everyone it touches. People live here for a few months but hang on to the memories for their whole lives; others come here for school and never leave; and some plan their lives so that they end up here.

Ann Arbor would not exist if not for Elisha Rumsey and John Allen. The two men first met in Detroit in 1824, far from their respective homes. It turned out that both had very good reasons for leaving their pasts behind. In Virginia, Allen's father left him with financial troubles that could not be resolved. Knowing that he needed to earn cash quickly and being aware that the government was offering cheap land out west, Allen gathered some belongings and headed out of town in the fall of 1823, leaving his second wife and new baby behind. After attempts to make money in Baltimore and Buffalo failed, he kept going until he ended up in Detroit, where he made the acquaintance of Elisha Walker Rumsey.

Rumsey is believed to be from New York, although some sources say he might have originally been from Connecticut. History records that Rumsey may have left New York for economic reasons, personal gossip (he reportedly lived with his wife before marriage) or both. For the second time in his life, Rumsey found himself in Detroit in early 1824.

When the two men met, Allen presented his idea of using cash on hand to buy land, sell off the lots and make some quick and easy money. They got a one-horse sleigh and headed west.

Village map, around 1836. *Bentley Historical Library.*

On a cold day in February, Elisha Rumsey and John Allen found a clearing in the forest near the Huron River. In May, the two traveled to nearby Wayne County and registered the plat for Annarbour. Allen paid $600 for 480 acres, Rumsey $200 for 160 acres. Within a month, a house stood at the corner of what are now Huron and First Streets and the story of Ann Arbor began.

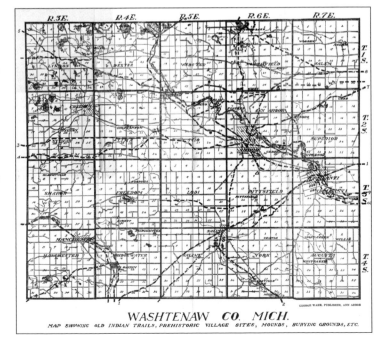

Above:
Warranty
deed between
John Allen
and Ann Allen
and James
Kingsley,
1834. *Bentley
Historical
Library.*

Right: County
map of Native
American
tribes. *Bentley
Historical
Library.*

Today, over 120,000 people live in Ann Arbor. We are home to a world-class university, exquisite dining establishments and arts and culture that provide entertainment every day of the year. We are consistently ranked at or near the top of "smartest cities in America" lists and "best places to live" surveys. There is little doubt that our future is very bright.

But we also have a past that must not be forgotten. Stories of businesses, events and people who shaped the city must not be lost. Some of those stories are in the pages that follow; many more are yet to be written.

Authors' Note: Given our town's long and illustrious history, there is no way we could include every single business and building that existed. We hope you will be generous and enjoy the memories contained in this book. And if we didn't cover your favorite spot? Well, that just means we'll have to do a sequel!

1

WELCOME TO ANN ARBOR!

From Bloody Corners to East Ann Arbor, We've Got a Place for You!

BLOODY CORNERS

Early Ann Arbor must have been a lovely sight—burr oaks all around the town, arbors full of ripe grapes, the gentle tinkle of the creek flowing past First and Huron Streets…and that bright red house called "Bloody Corners!"

Our early settlers had to live somewhere. For them, however, "somewhere" did not exist until they built it. Two of our own founders, Elisha and Mary "Ann" Rumsey, used heavy logs to build their abode on Huron Street near First Street. The little blockhouse greeted many newcomers to our town. At various times, the home was used as a tavern, hotel and coffeehouse, as well as the residence of the Rumseys. Eventually, it became known as the Washtenaw Coffee House and was the must-see spot for all those passing through or moving in.

John Allen took a little more time to build his homestead. His wife, Ann, was not with him, so he slept in an overturned carriage for a bit. But eventually, the missus was on her way, and he had to start building. Allen nestled into the northwest corner of what are now Main and Huron Streets. For reasons one can only imagine, he thought it would be a magnificent idea to paint his two-story log blockhouse a bright shade of red, and the home was quickly dubbed Bloody Corners.

Eventually, Ann Allen showed up into town. Her reaction to her new home is lost to the ages; nonetheless, she and other members of the Allen family all hunkered down in Bloody Corners. At various times, the building also

Right: John Allen. *Bentley Historical Library.*

Below: Masonic Block, one of the many clusters of buildings that replaced John Allen's abode at Huron and Main Streets. *Bentley Historical Library.*

Franklin House, a hotel located at the northwest corner of Huron and Main Streets. *Bentley Historical Library.*

housed a tavern and a store. It was also the place where the first Masonic lodge in the area was founded in 1827.

In 1850, Allen took off to find gold in the western United States; his wife left for her home in Virginia shortly thereafter. In the later part of the 1850s, the little red house was replaced by the Franklin House, a multistory hotel. The space then became the Gregory Block in 1862. That block hosted banks, bars, offices and other necessities of life in the late 1800s. The taverns that existed at the location include the Orient, Dot's Bar and the Star Bar. In 1982, Joe Tiboni opened Joe's Star Lounge at the spot. The large building that is there now is called One North Main and houses high-end condominiums and offices.

FOCUS ON ANN ALLEN

Two men get credit for founding our town. To be sure, they were the adventurers who came west to find their homestead. But attention must be given to the women who followed them, who added immeasurable things to our town and who left their mark in their own way.

Born in Staunton, Virginia, on January 22, 1797, Ann Arbor's future founding mother was named Agnes Barry. Nine days after her birth, her mother died from complications stemming from the delivery. Agnes's father was overwhelmed by his wife's death and reportedly begged his family to come over from Ireland to help him. They were not able to, so he hired a local young woman to care for his daughter. When Agnes was just three years old, two things happened to her: her father passed away, and her family began calling her Ann Isabella after her late mother.

Ann's loving aunt, uncle and grandmother groomed the only child to be the Southern lady her parents wanted her to be and that her inheritance made possible. At sixteen, Ann married a gentleman farmer and doctor named William McCue. Five years later, McCue was dead, leaving Ann a widowed mother of their two sons.

Founding mother Ann Allen did not like the town, possibly because she was used to much finer living in Virginia. *Bentley Historical Library.*

At the age of twenty-one, Ann moved in with her deceased husband's brother and his wife. At twenty-four, Ann married her second husband, John Allen, a twenty-five-year-old Scotch-Irish widower who also had two children. The marriage was described as one of convenience, partly because of the very different personalities of the people involved in it. John was an extrovert, very self-confident and friendly. Ann, on the other hand, was shy, private and introverted. Nevertheless, the two wed on June 7, 1821, and Ann immediately moved to Allen's farm; her two sons remained with their uncle and aunt. Their only child, Sarah, born on May 10, 1823, was named after Ann's grandmother.

In the fall of 1823, John Allen took off for Baltimore, Buffalo and finally Michigan. After John's departure, Ann returned to her former brother-in-law's home to reside with Sarah and her two older sons. At this point, the boys' uncle, concerned about John Allen's financial troubles, convinced a court to give him guardianship over them.

In August 1824, Ann received a letter from the Michigan Territory. In it were instructions on how to join John in the new settlement he'd cofounded and named Annarbour. John's plan was for Ann, Sarah, John's two children from his first marriage and John's parents to travel to Annarbour by covered wagon. But what of Ann's two sons from her first marriage? Heartbreakingly, Ann's wealthy former brother-in-law asserted his guardianship over his nephews and demanded that they remain in Virginia. Ann is reported to have felt extremely guilty, even though she had no control over the situation.

Ripped away from the comforts she had grown up with, Ann now faced life as a frontier wife. It is fair to say that she was not prepared for this. Ann grew up in the South. She was wealthy. Her family owned slaves. She received the benefits of slave labor and avoided household chores and tasks. Perhaps because of this, she was not the hearty "pioneer woman" people have grown used to seeing in movies and on television. She had to deal not only with a rough frontier town but also with the misery of having left her two sons behind in Virginia.

At first, Ann had some comfort from her husband's increased wealth. She had a pleasant (albeit bright red) home, servants and nice clothes; however, the financial panic of 1837 drove the Allens into poverty.

Hints of Ann's depression can be found in a letter she sent to her son in Virginia in 1837. She wrote: "When I look back, all that I had is gone to the four winds; when I look forward, all is darkness." At the time, of course, clinical depression was not well understood, and there were no services to aid Ann.

Help finally arrived in the form of her son Thomas McCue, who came to Ann Arbor in 1844 and fetched his mother and half sister. Ann spent the rest of her life in her home state, enduring the Civil War and its aftermath. Sadly, personal devastation continued to haunt Ann—both of her sons died young. Ann herself passed away at her daughter's home in New Hope, Virginia, on November 27, 1875.

The Rumseys

Just as little is known about our town's founding mother Ann Allen, there is likewise scant information about our other founding family: Mary Ann (who went by "Ann") and Elisha Rumsey. As previously noted, Elisha resided in New York just prior to meeting John Allen. It was there that he met Ann, believed to be a widow when she met Elisha. No pictures of the two have ever been discovered. While we don't know much about their daily lives in

Ann Arbor, a publication called *Godey's Lady's Book* provides a small glimpse of Ann Rumsey.

Described in *Ann Arbor Yesterdays* as "a glorified fashion magazine of the mid-1800s," *Godey's* featured poetry, engravings and articles by prominent women of the era. In the spring of 1852, a writer named Mrs. E.F. Ellet curated an article using essays written by the headmistress of the Clark School for Girls, Mary Clark. "The Pioneer Mothers of Michigan" described Ann Rumsey as a woman "of a remarkable and distinguished appearance and of energetic character and commanding aspect" with "a cheerful disposition, a disregard of hardships, and a resolute way of making the best of everything." The essay quoted John Allen as saying Ann Rumsey was "always ready with good humor and a good supper."

Although Mary Clark's essays spoke of the mother of John Allen—who apparently received sixteen offers of marriage when she was eighteen and was "eminently handsome" at the age of seventy-six—it said little about Ann Allen. *Ann Arbor's Yesterdays* suggests that this might be because she was still living when the articles were published. We do learn that Mary Clark believed Ann Rumsey to have entered the town "with a ready spirit of enterprise" and that she and her husband were well-to-do, bringing "horses and other stock" with them to Ann Arbor.

Sadly, there is not much more known about the Rumseys. Elisha passed away in 1827, and Ann soon remarried and moved to Indiana, where she is presumed to have spent her remaining years.

MALLETTS CREEK SETTLEMENT/EAST ANN ARBOR

Some of the roads in Ann Arbor tell you where you will end up if you drive far enough. For example, Ann Arbor–Saline Road runs between those two cities, Dexter–Ann Arbor Road takes you from one city to the other and so on. It might then come as a surprise to see a road that goes to Milan but is called Platt Road. As it turns out, Ann Arborites are nothing if not helpful and at one time did call that road Milan. This was back in the days of East Ann Arbor, which was a completely different municipality from the city of Ann Arbor in its time.

The Potawatomi tribe initially inhabited the area bounded by Packard and Milan (Platt) Road; however, in 1807, the United States brokered the Treaty of Detroit and forced several indigenous nations to give up their lands. As part of the treaty, the Potawatomi received $1,666.66 up front and $400.00 each year after for relinquishing to white settlers the area that would initially be known as the Malletts Creek Settlement and later called East Ann Arbor.

School

The first non-Native settlers arrived around 1825, just a year after Elisha Rumsey and John Allen settled Ann Arbor proper. The McDowell family and the Whitmore family received land patents for an area just east of where Packard and Platt Roads meet today.

It was in this wilderness, under an oak tree, that the first school in Washtenaw County convened. Initially, this outdoor school was in session only during the summer months; however, settlers soon built a log-cabin school southeast of Packard and Platt Roads. They called this the Mallet Creek School, and it held indoor classes from 1825 until 1853.

An elementary school opened at the corner of Carpenter and Packard Streets as a one-room log-cabin schoolhouse in 1825. It became known as Carpenter School in 1837. The school moved to the west side of Carpenter Road in 1854 and to 3360 Carpenter Road in 1914; at this latter location, the building was wired for electricity, becoming the first school in the area to do so. The school moved to the building it currently occupies in 1952 and has the honor of having educated students in the same geographical area for 193 years.

In the mid-1850s, Dr. Benajah Ticknor leased a triangle of his land at what is now Packard Street and Stone School Road with the express intention of building a school. In 1854, the first Stone School was built, remaining until 1911, when residents built a larger school that educated children until 1949. The school remains standing, housing the Stone School Cooperative Preschool since 1955.

Around 1925, parents expressed concern about having their children walk up Packard Street to the two schools. The committee formed to address the issue considered a variety of ideas, ultimately opting to form its own district separate from Carpenter and Stone Schools. After voters approved this idea, District Number Nine, Pittsfield Township, was born.

One of the first decisions to be made was where to put the new school. To that end, W.H. Rohde deeded to the new district four lots located between Platt Road and Rosedale Street, just south of Packard Street. Erected in 1926, the Platt School, named after local farmer and landowner Henry

Platt, thrived and eventually added on rooms and a basement as its student population grew.

In 1944, the Noble-Grandmont Corporation purchased a tract of land east of District Nine; this area became Pittsfield Village, a condominium community that was eventually annexed into the city and continues to flourish with lovely open green spaces. After purchasing this land, the Noble-Grandmont Corporation marked five acres on Pittsfield Boulevard for use for a school and subsequently deeded the land to the government. Originally known as School Number Two in District Number Nine in Pittsfield Township, it is now familiar to its neighborhood as Pittsfield Elementary School, part of the Ann Arbor School District.

By the early 1950s, the Platt School had closed. It later served as a music store, a plumber's shop and ultimately a church. While being used as the Greater Faith Christian Center Church, the building burned down in 2002.

Church

East Ann Arbor held interdenominational church services at the local school on Sundays beginning in 1926. Its services boasted about ninety to one hundred attendees per week, led by a local engineer named Ivan Cuthbert. A parent-teacher organization and a women's club prospered, and both groups hosted such events as carnivals, banquets and talent nights. In addition to being social groups, they also believed in doing good charity works. They sponsored other organizations, raised money for a variety of causes and purchased gifts for patients at the Washtenaw County Infirmary.

Retail

In the 1920s and 1930s, a number of retail establishments served East Ann Arbor. McMillan's Grocery was at the northeast corner of Packard and Platt Roads, while Read's Variety Store (later Buster's Market) occupied the southwest corner of the intersection. Behind the store were gasoline and kerosene pumps, along with an icehouse. Across Platt Road was the East Ann Arbor Shopping Center, which contained the East Ann Arbor Food Market, W.W. Ladd Dry Goods, the Lundy hardware store and Community Drug.

Also on the southwest corner of Packard Street and Platt Road was the Ypsi-Ann interurban railway station. The line began service along Packard Street (also known as South Road or Electric Line Road) in 1891. It

Pencil drawings of Sherman Hinckley's farm. The bottom image is a sketch of the Washtenaw County Poor House, located at Washtenaw and Platt Roads. *Bentley Historical Library.*

eventually extended east to Detroit, west to Jackson and south to Milan along Platt/Milan Road. The interurban line declared bankruptcy and folded in the 1920s, but the station building remained. Its subsequent uses would include East Ann Arbor's administration building, a police department and a barbershop. It was finally removed in the mid-1950s.

Cemeteries

As the settlers celebrated life, they also had to acknowledge and honor death. East Ann Arbor had at least four cemeteries, including Crittenden, at Bemis and Carpenter Roads; Harwood, at the southeast corner of Textile and Campbell Roads (which had the distinction of having the first recorded burial); and the Old Negro Burying Ground, which was south of Ellsworth Road and east of Carpenter Road. While there are no remains of these cemeteries, current occupants of Ann Arbor can visit the fourth cemetery, Terhune Pioneer Cemetery, by going up a flight of steps in the Forestbrooke neighborhood.

Services

Located at the intersection of Washtenaw and Platt Roads, the Washtenaw County Poor House and Insane Asylum opened in 1837 and functioned as a farm where residents grew their own food. The building was razed forty years later and replaced by a brick infirmary, which closed in 1971. After the infirmary was demolished in 1979, the county developed the site as County Farm Park and opened the Meri Lou Murray Recreation Center on a corner of the site twelve years later.

City Services

In 1947, East Ann Arbor became a city, necessitating city services for its two thousand residents. Nearby Pittsfield Township could not provide police or fire protection, so the city built its own fire department behind the shopping center on Platt Road and used the interurban line building for its police station, as noted above. While these services were easily provided, water and sewer service proved to be cost-prohibitive. The only reasonable solution was annexation to the city of Ann Arbor. In November 1956, East Ann Arbor was annexed into the city by a two-to-one vote in East Ann Arbor and a three-to-one vote in the city.

2

EATING AND DRINKING

From Nathan Drake's Saloon & Eating House to Drake's Sandwich Shop

Saloons

When Germans helped to settle Ann Arbor, they brought with them their love of beer and talent for brewing. To be fair, non-German settlers also likely enjoyed their malted barley and hops, and lucky for them all, they had plenty of places to imbibe. Dozens of saloons dotted the landscape of young Ann Arbor; one report says that almost fifty saloons were in operation by the early 1870s!

The 1872 volume of the *Cole & Keating's Ann Arbor Directory* listed establishments by names of the proprietors: George Guntkunst at 4 West Washington Street, Christian Sanzi in the Bucholz Block, William Saunders at 5 Broadway Street, John Kettner at 20 East Washington Street, Charles Binder's Saloon at 4 West Liberty Street (now the Alley Bar), John Laughlin on Depot Street between Pontiac (now Beakes) Street and Fifth Avenue, William Wallace on Fourth Avenue between Huron and Washington Streets, Morris Lucas at the corner of Fourth Avenue and Catherine Street, George Lutz at 40 South Main Street, Gottlieb Frey at 11 Washington Street, Henry Binder's "billiard, lager beer, and refreshment saloon" at 51 South Main Street, John Haupt at 11 East Liberty Street, Franz Nebel at 7 North Main Street, George Bauer at 22 Broadway Street, John Henrich on Fourth Avenue between Washington and Huron Streets, Anson Besimer on Huron Street between Main Street and Second Avenue

Drake's saloon and eating house on the Courthouse Square. *Bentley Historical Library.*

Charles Binder's saloon, around 1880 (where Alley Bar is now). *Bentley Historical Library.*

(now Ashley Street), Nathan Drake's "saloon and eating house" at 20 East Huron Street on the Courthouse Square, John Clair on Ann Street between Main Street and Fourth Avenue, George Weidelich on Washington Street between Main Street and Second Avenue, John Albrecht's "bakery and saloon" on Pontiac (Beakes) Street between Fifth Avenue and Summit Street, William Exinger at the corner of Detroit and Pontiac (Beakes) Streets, and Frederick Rentschler at 40 Liberty Street. Another interesting item listed in the 1872 directory is that at least two women worked in the saloons: Mrs. Bicer worked at a saloon at the corner of Fifth Avenue and Pontiac (Beakes) Street, and Mrs. Margaret Diehl worked at a saloon at Detroit and Fuller Streets.

While much of the history of these saloon owners and their bars was not preserved, there are some stories that can and must be told. One concerns a night in 1856 when Jacob Hangsterfer (proprietor of Hangsterfer's Hall at Main and Washington Streets) insisted that a couple of rowdy students leave his establishment after he turned down their demands for free beer. In response, they broke open kegs of beer and destroyed property. Next, they crashed a private event at Henry Binder's Hotel and Saloon, gulping

Hangsterfer Hall, on the southwest corner of Main and Washington Streets, was torn down in 1926 when a new Kresge building was built on the site. *Bentley Historical Library.*

down the drinks that were set out on the bar. Binder managed to catch one of the boys, but the others ran out, returning with more friends and weapons, including battering rams. When Binder's walls started to collapse, he released his dog on them, but the boys set off their own dogs, who killed Binder's poor pooch. When the boys left to get the muskets they used in military drills, Binder let his captive go.

Although warrants were issued for the young men involved, both faculty and fellow students shielded them such that Binder eventually withdrew his complaint. This withdrawal also might have been prompted by threats of charges of selling beer to minors (although whether Binder actually "sold" the beer seems in dispute).

Though no criminal charges resulted from this occurrence, it is the event that led to Division Street taking on a more literal meaning, as a gentlemen's agreement decreed that no liquor licenses would be allowed east of Division. The arrangement became formal in 1903 through an act of common council.

BREWERIES

The breweries of yesteryear were different from the brewpubs and taprooms that people are familiar with today. The former were businesses where brewers made beer; visitors did not drop in and buy a pint, hang out with friends and socialize. Employees put the beer into barrels, and the barrels were then taken by horse-drawn wagon to local saloons. While brewers and workers likely enjoyed mugs at work, these were places of business and not pubs.

In 1861, there were three breweries in Ann Arbor: Hooper's (at State and Fuller Streets from 1858 to 1866), the Bavarian (which operated on Fuller Street between Elizabeth and State Streets from 1860 to 1872) and the City Brewery. The former two were considered small home operations, as opposed to the City Brewery, which was bigger and more commercially successful.

Things changed when a man named Peter Brehm arrived in Ann Arbor and started the Western Brewery at 416 Fourth Street in 1861. The Western Brewery focused on lager—the light, accessible beer that dominated America's palate before the modern rise of craft brewing. The success of the brewery made Brehm a wealthy man. He purchased the land at 326 West Liberty Street, tore down the existing structure and built a mansion in the Second Empire style.

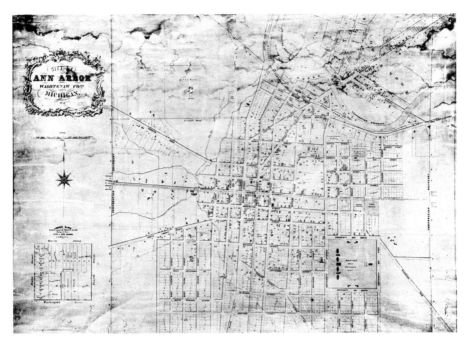

The 1853 map of Ann Arbor indicates "brewery" at 206–222 South First Street. The first city directory named the brewery as G.F. Hauser's City Brewery. *Bentley Historical Library.*

Three years after Brehm's completion of his magnificent home, the Panic of 1873 hit. Banks failed, the New York Stock Exchange closed for ten days, businesses laid off employees and railroad construction and new building efforts stopped. Many breweries both locally and nationwide were caught up in the economic depression, but the Western Brewery continued, albeit under different ownership.

History is silent as to why Brehm lost control of the brewery just prior to the panic. However, it is known that he suffered from what the newspapers described as "mania" or "melancholy." This may have been brought on by clinical depression or alcoholism, but such mental health issues were not publicly discussed at the time. Sadly, Brehm came home one day in 1873, told his wife he was being sued and started off toward the courthouse. At some point, he returned to his room and died from a gunshot wound to the head. Newspaper reports were kind to Brehm, saying he was "a kind-hearted and very generous man, respected by all who knew him."

Shortly after the Western Brewery opened, the Northern Brewery (at 1037 Jones Drive from 1872 to 1909; this building is now known as the Tech

City Brewery/Central Mills building. *Bentley Historical Library.*

Brewery) and the Central Brewery (at 724 North Fifth Avenue from 1865 to 1875) began producing beer.

Central drew its water from a spring near the house that its owner, John Alan Volz, built next door. It enjoyed some good times prior to the Panic of 1873, when Volz was forced to sell to Jacob Beck. Under Beck, Central Brewery went on to operate until the late 1870s, at which time breweries all over the country were declining in number. The economic depression after the panic combined with local prohibition laws forced many brewers to close up shop. The Central Brewery building later became the Ann Arbor Pop Works, where Bert Stoll made ginger ale and root beer; it then served as home to Ross and Welch's Bottling Works. After that, the building at 724 North Fifth Avenue housed German immigrants, Italian immigrants and later Japanese Americans released from detainment camps after the end of World War II. It is now an apartment complex called Brewery Apartments.

As a side note, the tunnels under the former Central Brewery have been cause for discussion since the 1970s. When construction workers renovated a building at Summit Street and North Fifth Avenue, they found vaults and parts of a tunnel system that observers speculated might extend to the nearby Michigan Central railroad tracks. Firefighters later unearthed subbasements in several buildings on Depot Street near the apartments. David

Byrd, then director of the Ann Arbor Community Development Center, told the *Ann Arbor News* that slaves may have been transported through these underground systems on their flight to freedom, with the end of the line being in the former Central Brewery. He indicated plans to open up an on-site museum to preserve these underground vaults. However, a 1990s article in the *Observer* indicated that no evidence ever proved that these underground caverns were used for anything other than storing beer.

Situated on Traver Creek, Northern Brewery was opened by George Krause in 1872. Twelve years later, Herman Hardinghaus took over the running of the brewery and built a new brick building for his endeavors as well as his own home, known as the brewmaster's house, right next door. Although biographers praised Hardinghaus's ale as "superior," the brewery didn't survive Prohibition. A later owner named Ernest Rehberg brewed beer until about 1908 before converting to an ice business. Meanwhile, Hardinghaus moved on to Ypsilanti to become a partner in L.Z. Foerster & Company Brewers.

After founder Peter Brehm's death, Christian Martin and Matthias Fischer bought Western Brewery, keeping the name and carrying on the business of brewing beer. In 1903, new owners named it the Michigan Union Brewery, because most of the employees were represented by a local union. By 1906, it was the last brewery left in town; ultimately, it turned out to be the only

Central Brewery building. *Ann Arbor District Library.*

one to survive Prohibition, which started in 1918 in Michigan. It did what many other breweries did during that time—rented to an ice cream maker. After the "noble experiment" failed and the Twenty-First Amendment went into effect, three partners, including Peter Brehm's son Gustave, took over and reopened as Ann Arbor Brewing Company.

It was a well-known secret that customers could go into the back of Michigan Union Brewery, fill up a stein and drink a beer for free. They could choose from Cream Top ale, Old-Tyme ale and Town Club; however, these were all the same beer! The only different ale the brewery produced was a springtime bock. While the beer was described by at least one resident as being only good to put out fires with, the brewery stayed open until 1949.

RESURGENCE OF BREWERIES IN ANN ARBOR

At one point in history, every small town has its share of breweries. In the 1870s, Ann Arbor had about eight thousand residents and six or seven breweries. As refrigeration proliferated and goods became mass marketed, more and more people began drinking national brands instead of regional ones. And Prohibition did not help—over 1,300 breweries existed in 1916, but only a small percentage survived those "dry" years.

The summer of 1995 proved to be a banner one for brewpubs in Ann Arbor when Arbor Brewing Company and Grizzly Peak opened on Washington Street; both businesses continue to thrive as of this writing.

While a number of brewpubs opened and closed in the 1990s, one lost brewpub continues to be fondly remembered by its patrons: Leopold Bros. The brewpub and distillery on Main Street opened in 1999 in a factory that dated back a century. (The building remains and is home to Criteo.) Todd and Scott Leopold aimed to make their beer and their business as environmentally friendly as possible—pub tables were built from reused materials, the water management system reduced waste water and a greenhouse was built in the back of the building. In addition to their award-winning beers, they distilled a number of spirits in house. While the brewpub in Ann Arbor is closed, the Leopold brothers continue to craft alcohol in Colorado.

Another brewery called Brewbakers Craft Brewery and Bakehouse operated in the late 1990s in the Kerrytown Market. While it did not have a taproom, it did have homemade bread and freshly brewed beer for takeout.

BEER BREVITIES

Many of the old newspapers had a column where local residents could share news of where they had visited, who was in town, illnesses and recoveries and reports of social events—a kind of Facebook for the 1880s. In Ann Arbor, the column was called Brevities and provides some interesting tales of goings-on at various bars and saloons.

Some were sad, such as the one that reported that Richard Flannary died on November 1, 1874, after a fight at his saloon at Main and Catherine Streets. The perpetrators included Joseph Audett, Hiram Pickard, Peter Hanlon, John Norton, Jethro Maybe and "two strangers." Flannary left his wife widowed with three small children. The first criminal trial ended with a hung jury, but the second jury convicted Jethro Maybe for manslaughter.

Many brevities were strictly about business. In 1873, the common council requested a report of all saloon owners who had not paid their license fee and reported that a woman was operating a saloon "near the depot" without a license. A year later, saloon keepers were "stirred up" when they received postcards signed "Many Ladies" who demanded saloon prayer meetings. In 1893, Mayor Bradley Thompson vetoed an ordinance that would have allowed saloons to stay open past 10:30 p.m. in the summer months. It was not expected that the common council would be able to override this veto.

Some were a little more lighthearted, such as the man who, while being dragging to jail, offered to buy the policeman a glass of beer if the officer let him go. The policeman said it was the "severest test of virtue" he had faced, but he overcame temptation and threw the man in jail.

TAVERNS FROM THE PAST

Ann Arborites have many different bars about which to reminisce. Some may be out of the memory of current residents, such as Drake's Saloon on the Courthouse Square or the Cupid Bar (popular in the 1940s, this spot later became the Flame). A few might recall the Court Tavern, a bar at 108

East Huron Street that opened as the Court Café and was one of the first businesses in town to reopen as a bar after the ratification of the Twenty-First Amendment; it lasted from 1933 until 1966. But then there are some legendary bars that we may not remember but that were very well known in their day. At the corner of Fourth Avenue and Ann Street, one now finds the Ann Arbor Running Company. A few years ago, one would have found the beloved Kaleidoscope bookstore; many years ago, one would have found Joe Parker's Saloon. No matter what business is on this corner, customers always see the cursive "Joe" written in tile as they walk inside. The "Joe" was Joe Parker, owner and proprietor of the saloon that bore his name. Once a home to the prominent Chapin family, the building became the Arlington Hotel in the 1890s. The 1908 Polk's Directory lists Misters Stark and Dawes as the owners; the hotel offered steam heat in the rooms and only cost $1.50 per day. The hotel then changed names and owners to become the Catalpa Hotel, and in 1913, it became home to Joe Parker's Saloon.

Originally located at 204 South Main Street (at same spot but not same building as the former Café Felix), Joe's served as a well-loved lunch counter and saloon. After that building was demolished, Joe moved operations to the Catalpa.

According to a *Michigan Daily* article in 1946, Joe had some rules: no freshmen allowed (they went to Gus's Place), he did not allow you to get drunk (and to that end, Joe kept people on beer as best he could, trying to avoid hard liquor) and if you got too rowdy, Joe would throw you out. This bar, like most others of its time, served only men, as women who drank in public were not considered "ladies." It was said that Joe would lock his door before he let a woman inside.

While the bar is immortalized in the song "I Want to Go Back to Michigan," it only lasted in brick-and-mortar form until Prohibition. Also likely leading to its closure was a "blue law" enacted in 1907 and finally enforced in 1913; the law held that no liquor could be served to students, and a bar's license would be revoked if it violated the law. Joe's bar served mostly students (except freshmen), as townies avoided it and drank with university faculty at the Town and Gown Club. The Ann Arbor Chamber of Commerce purchased the building after the last drink at the iconic Joe's, but the name is still there for passersby to see.

Many more recent taverns elicit memories and stories today. While this list is not exhaustive, it hopefully ignites some happy recollections for past and current Ann Arbor townies: the Lab (144 Hill Street, a basement club featuring all-ages shows), Odyssey (Huron Street), Village Bell (South

Demolition of Parker's Saloon building on Main Street. *Bentley Historical Library.*

University), Mitch's Place and Touchdown Café (both at 1220 South University Avenue, now the Blue Leprechaun), Annie's Dugout (a bar and lounge at 2324 Dexter Avenue, where Knight's Steakhouse is now), Derby Bar (113 East Ann Street), Clint's Club (111 East Ann Street), Dooley's (310 Maynard Street, where Scorekeepers is), the Liberty Inn (one of the many bars at 112 West Liberty Street, where the Alley Bar is now), Mackinac Jack's (217 South Ashley Street), Primo's Showbar (the rock and roll dance club that replaced Mackinac Jack's and where Bob Seger performed in his early years), People's Ballroom (community operated, nonprofit home of rock and roll at 502 East Washington Street), the Midway Bar (Ann

Mackinac Jack's. *Bentley Historical Library.*

Blue Frogge. *Bentley Historical Library.*

Street), the Quality Bar (347 South Main Street, which was previously home to the Quality Bakery—the owners simply removed the k, e and y to form the sign), Touchdown Café, the Town Bar (a jazz club located at 212 East Huron Street), Golden Falcon (a jazz club on Fourth Street that later became Maude's), Studio 4 (where Maude's was, now a Ruth's Chris Steak House), the Full Moon and the Crow Bar (South Main Street), Goodnight Gracie's (301 West Huron Street, now the Last Word), Cafe Habana (211 East Washington Street), Live at PJs (102 South First Street), the Blue Frogge (a dance club frequented by Madonna at 611 Church Street, now Rick's American Café), the Schwaben Inn (215 South Ashley Street), the Stadium Tavern (at Liberty Street and Stadium Boulevard, previously Tice's Tavern), Evergreen Tavern (on Dexter Avenue west of Maple Road), Toni's Apartment Supper Club (in Huron Towers; the Lunch Room Bakery & Cafe there now), the Scene (which took over the space that had been the Rubaiyat at 102 South First Street), Cubs AC (1950 South Industrial Highway), Village Pub (3452 Washtenaw Avenue), Pawly's Tavern (120 West Liberty Street) and the Fifth Quarter (210 South Fifth Avenue).

PRETZEL BELL

There are many stories about how the "P-Bell" hosted both town and gown as students crowded to take their first legal drink and townies gathered to listen to the RFD Boys on Saturday nights. While pictures of the good ol' days show people imbibing and partying, some more serious things happened at the famed bar and restaurant as well.

In 1940, students filed a lawsuit against the Pretzel Bell over its refusal to serve customers who were African American. According to the *Michigan Daily*, the suit went nowhere, and some of the students involved were asked not to return to campus for the 1940 fall term.

In 1969, the Pretzel Bell suffered damage from a fire that destroyed Martin Haller's Department Store. Owner Clint Castor did his best to rescue the beloved University of Michigan memorabilia from the walls. Just four years after the fire, three criminals broke into Clint Castor's home. They demanded money, tied up Castor and his wife and pistol-whipped him. When told that the money was at the restaurant, two of the criminals drove Castor to the Pretzel Bell. After getting $1,500, they shoved him back into his car and talked about killing their captive.

A crowded Pretzel Bell. *Bentley Historical Library.*

Castor jumped from the car and phoned police. All three suspects were later apprehended.

In 1973, the Republican city council refused to endorse a resolution in support of Gay Pride Week. In response, about seventy people picketed city council, councilmembers' homes and the Pretzel Bell, where some Republicans were having dinner. That same year, a group called Ann Arbor Tomorrow (AAT) investigated the possibility of running a "shoppers' shuttle" between Main and State Street. Part of this shuttle would have run in the alley between the Pretzel Bell and Hutzel's before it turned around and went back.

Alas, unpaid employee withholding taxes resulted in the IRS seizing the assets of the restaurant. On the day the restaurant closed, folks lined up in the rain to bid on the auction selling off its assets. Most of the memorabilia and fixtures were auctioned off in 1985, including the namesake bell. An establishment with the same name but not otherwise connected to the original bar and restaurant operates on Main Street today.

DEL RIO

Every now and again, a place opens in the right spot at the right time. Even years after that place closes, people still remember the food, the waitstaff, the people, the drinks and the experience. For Ann Arbor, that time was 1970 and that place was the Del Rio.

It started with the idea that workers—waitstaff, bartenders and people who worked the door—could manage themselves by consensus. That idea led to over three decades of good times for countless townies and a place that an *Ann Arbor News* restaurant reviewer called "a way of life."

The Del Rio sat on the corner of Washington and Ashley Streets (where the Grizzly Den is now) in a neighborhood that was at best described as rough, featuring frequent patrols by police officers with lights and sirens blaring. The 1869-era building previously housed several German American restaurants, including Flautz's and Metzger's; a blacksmith shop; a bottling shop; and a hotel; by 1955, it was home to a hard-liquor bar with country music blaring from jukeboxes.

In the late 1960s, the neighborhood began to change with the opening of the Blind Pig and Mr. Flood's Party (now home of the West End Grill). In 1970, musician Rick Burgess and entrepreneur Ernie Harburg bought the place, changed the atmosphere (with a group of friends, they ripped paneling off the wall at 1:00 a.m. and opened at 8:00 p.m. the same day) and transformed the corner of Washington and Ashley Streets into a legendary and beloved bar.

There were reports of some initial discord between the clientele from the previous bar and the newer customers, the latter of whom tended to mirror the counterculture of Ann Arbor. Further problems arose when a disastrous first manager failed to pay taxes or keep the books; this ultimately led to the owners giving managerial duties to their staff. Workers took over the responsibilities of the former manager and eventually decided they didn't need one, leading to the management-by-consensus model that would carry the Del Rio for decades.

The inside was as eclectic as the clientele. The Del Rio displayed a collection of more than one thousand cassette tapes behind the bar; had a bottle of Mrs. Butterworth syrup next to the liquor (and they would make you finish the shot if you ordered it); featured live, free jazz on Sunday evenings; only accepted cash; referred to waiters and waitresses as the gender-neutral "wait"; and served everything from burritos to homemade soup to the Det Burger (a burger soaked in beer and topped with black olives and mushrooms,

Shakey Jake Woods stands outside the Del Rio. *Bentley Historical Library.*

Del Rio. *Bentley Historical Library.*

named after the cook who created it). The Del was run by staff who all shared in the profits equally and who all had an equal say in how it operated and in who was hired and fired. The bartenders had complete control over the music choice and volume. The chefs created the daily specials and were responsible for everything that went on in the kitchen, just as if they were cooking at home. The Del also featured poetry readings and art by local visual artists; it was called "home" by both establishment and anti-establishment.

And it all worked—until it didn't. Time marched on in counterculture Ann Arbor, and eventually, so did the Del Rio. A switch to more traditional management happened, and longtime employees either quit or were fired; some of these employees led a picket line out front. The Del went out with a bang with a celebration that began on New Year's Eve 2003 and lasted into the new year.

While many townies mention the Del Rio as their most missed bar, others had just as strong opinions on the other side. An *Ann Arbor News* reporter described it as "dark, yet…sun streaked…rude, yet it's inviting…a place to be alone and a place to be among friends." Some described it as having horrible service and being "insular," and complaints about the food were many. But ultimately, the Del Rio stood the test of time and served generations of townies, students and passersby through our town. Perhaps the best quote about the Del Rio is this: it wasn't for everyone, and that's just the way they wanted it.

THE BIRD OF PARADISE

Though jazz acts regularly featured at restaurants and bars around town, the Bird of Paradise was Ann Arbor's first club in a decade dedicated to jazz music when it debuted on Ashley Street in 1985. Ron Brooks, founder and proprietor, moved his eponymous trio from their regular engagement at the

Earle around the corner to play weekends, and he was soon able to welcome nationally known acts on the weekends and host regular engagements on weeknights with his own group and Ann Arbor's rich pool of local jazz talent. The *Ann Arbor News* called it "an elegance that isn't intimidating," with drinks "pricey, but strong." Enjoying the Sunday jazz brunch was one of coauthor Woodman's first tentative forays into acting like a grown-up.

In 2000, the Bird moved a block over to Main Street. An underground space beneath the Ark folk-music club promised to double the capacity, making the Bird much larger than even any of Detroit's jazz venues. It continued here for about four years. As it did with the first show, the Ron Brooks Trio headlined the Bird's last show on Tuesday, July 27, 2004. Brooks continued to headline and host music nights at other venues in the area, and the Southeast Michigan Jazz Association created an award in his name in 2012. Brooks still performs throughout the state.

OTHER NOTABLE PLACES

The Firefly Club continued to feature live jazz in the space the Bird of Paradise vacated on Ashley Street when it moved to Main Street in 2000. In 2007, the Firefly Club itself moved to South Main Street near Madison Street. It shared space with a performing arts school and hosted community groups and activities until its sudden closure in 2009.

The Fifth Dimension, which opened in 1966 at 218 West Huron Street, was a teen nightclub that boasted some of the biggest acts of the era: Jimi Hendrix, the Who, the Yardbirds, Procol Harum and Bob Seger were just some of the acts who graced the stage of the former bowling alley. The club endured until 1968 and later became the New Odyssey and then the Whiffletree restaurant.

Once called the Cupid Bar, the Flame Bar opened at 115 West Washington Street (now the site of the Logan restaurant) on April 30, 1949. A picture of Custer's Last Stand hung behind the bar, causing it to be nicknamed as such. It went on to become known as the city's first gay bar. (The Town Bar, located across the street, also attracted a LGBTQ crowd; however, history records the Flame as the city's first.) In 1972, up to sixty people gathered outside the bar to protest the exclusion of transgender persons and to request changes in the bar. Various groups demanded different things—more room to dance, no dress code, the end of discrimination against drag queens and an improved physical environment. These issues were resolved to varying degrees before the Flame closed in 1998.

In August 1974, a bar called Chances Are opened at 516 East Liberty Street. Bands such as Cheap Trick, Head East and Radio King rotated through in the early weeks, with national acts such as Stephen Stills and Bob Seger and the Silver Bullet Band appearing that fall. Renamed Second Chance after a dispute with a Chicago bar of the same name, the bar continued to sell out live shows until 1984, when it briefly closed and reopened as the Nectarine Ballroom. The *Ann Arbor News* reported on the change, saying that the new bar would be transformed into a "nightspot along the lines of New York's Red Parrot and Studio 54." The owners hoped to attract "yumpies—young upwardly mobile professionals," a reflection of changing times and changing demographics in the city. While the new spot would still feature live acts, DJs would also spin recorded music. The Nectarine remained in business until 2001; it has been the Necto Nightclub ever since.

Mr. Flood's Party has been described as the center of Ann Arbor culture in the 1970s and 1980s. It was opened in 1969 by the late Ned Duke and Buddy Jack at 120 West Liberty Street, the space currently occupied by the West End Grill. The bar featured live music seven nights a week, and locals could hear acts such as Commander Cody, the Prime Movers, George Bedard and the Bonnevilles, Dick Siegel and His Ministers of Melody and Mr. B.

In 1898, John Berger opened a saloon named the Bismark at 122 West Washington Street. He sold the business in 1917 to William Seagert, who then operated it during Prohibition (selling near beer, bitters and homebrewing products) and the Great Depression. In 1935, Richard Kearns bought the saloon and renamed it the Union Bar. The owners changed a few times until Jerry Pawlicki bought it and renamed it Old Town, a beloved townie institution that remains in business today.

Police knew a series of bars in the 100 block of East Ann Street as the "Block." Its reputation was as an area for rough bars and rough crowds, where heroin and other drugs could be easily obtained. A former police chief said, "In the early forties and fifties a call to Ann Street tickled your spine a little bit." But others remember it being known for its blues bars and for providing meeting spaces for African Americans. Two bars dominated the block: Clint's Club and the Derby Bar. At 111 East Ann Street, Clint's Club was a long, narrow space with a small bandstand. The Derby, located at 113 East Ann Street, was the scene of two murders in 1974. In the mid-

Mr. Flood's Party. *Bentley Historical Library.*

1970s, developers purchased the buildings and shut down the pool halls and the Derby Bar.

The spot at 109 North Main Street (now home to the multiuse One North Main development) served as home base for bars starting with the Orient at the turn of the century, Dot's Tavern and the Star Bar, ending its run as home to drinking establishments with Joe's Star Lounge. In the early 1980s, Joe Tiboni renovated and renamed the Star Bar. During its three-year run, Joe's Star Lounge entertained countless guests with its music and dance floor. Local and national acts such as Big Joe Turner, Commander Cody, Country Joe McDonald, REM, the Violent Femmes, Sonic Youth, Los Lobos, Dick Siegel and Steve Nardella all graced the stage.

The Wonder Bar was described by the *Ann Arbor News* as no-nonsense, no-frills and the last "Black bar in Ann Arbor," earning this name after the bars on the Block were shut down in 1975. At the time of its closing, patrons mourned its demise, telling the *Ann Arbor News* about the pool table, juke box, pinball machine and lively social atmosphere. One customer called it "more of a social hall than bar" and a "place to keep in touch with what's going on in the black community and [to] catch up." The owners transferred the liquor license to PanTree restaurant in 1982, and the Wonder Bar was no more.

SIT-DOWN RESTAURANTS

Few restaurants evoke such nostalgia and love as Drake's Sandwich Shop. Drake's was a fixture of North University Avenue, originally as a soda fountain and candy store. Drake's signature figure, Truman Tibbals, hired on as a dishwasher in 1926 and bought the restaurant outright in 1929. People remember Drake's for its fresh limeade, tuna sandwiches for under two dollars and the availability of Oreos as a side item. Drake's maintained its retro charm, cash-only policy and extremely affordable prices until 1993, when Tibbals began cancer treatment and his children made the difficult decision to close the restaurant. Ann Arbor police officers could often be found at Drake's, and Tibbals was made an honorary officer before his passing in 1994. When Drake's was dismantled, some of the booths were offered to the community. One went to Datastat, an Ann Arbor research firm, which installed the booth in its employee break room. Drake's North University Avenue space was quickly occupied by a coffee-and-bagel chain restaurant that has remained there ever since.

Argiero's was a family-owned Italian restaurant that rested comfortably on the edge of Kerrytown for forty years. It served pizza alongside more traditional Italian entrees and had a full bar. Its founder, Tony Argiero, passed away in 2016, and his family ran the restaurant for about another year before closing, without prior announcement, in 2017. Its distinctive flatiron building, at Detroit and Catherine Streets, is now occupied by the Detroit Street Filling Station.

The Village Bell, at 1321 South University Avenue, was the sister restaurant of the Pretzel Bell on Liberty Street. It was later replaced by the Chicago deep-dish restaurant Pizzeria Uno; like other restaurants in the chain, it focused on pizza and beer. Later, a short-lived club called the All-Star Café (no relation to the celebrity-owned Original All-Star Café) occupied the space. The location is currently Sadako Japanese Restaurant, while Pizzeria Uno is now common around Michigan, franchised as Uno Chicago Grill, a suburban casual dining chain that serves deep-dish pizza.

PanTree, located at Liberty and Division Streets where the Center for the Education of Women is now, opened in 1980 as the first and only twenty-four-hour restaurant in the downtown area. The *Ann Arbor News'* Constance Crump characterized it as a "California fern bar run amok," but it had a great location with a nice view of Liberty Plaza and was unique in catering to nighthawks. It also hosted live music. In 1986, it was renovated and introduced a bar called Annie's Arbor, but it still closed about a year

Drake's Sandwich Shop, never forgotten. *Bentley Historical Library.*

Young women at Drake's, around 1937. *Bentley Historical Library.*

later. After the PanTree closed, a franchise Denny's Restaurant moved in downtown and featured a bar. Though open twenty-four hours like other Denny's, it stopped serving alcohol at 2:00 a.m. in compliance with state law.

Steve Bellock, owner of the Seva vegetarian restaurant, purchased PanTree in early 1988, changing its name to Night Town on the Park. Despite the ownership, the new restaurant had a completely different menu from Seva, which was then in the same block but did not maintain the round-the-clock hours of PanTree. It opened in the late spring of 1988 after renovations and closed in October of the same year.

Farrell's was located in Briarwood Mall near the movie theater. An old-timey concept restaurant with elaborate ice cream sundaes and arcade games, Farrell's was a favored birthday-party destination for kids in the early 1980s with locations all over the United States. Farrell's relaunched in 2016 as a property of TV host and celebrity entrepreneur Marcus Lemonis and currently maintains two locations in Southern California.

Bimbo's Pizza, located on Washington Street and on Washtenaw Avenue (Bimbo's on the Hill), still evokes many happy memories for townies. Families in the 1960s remember Bimbo's for its thin-crust pizza, 1930s

Seva in 1971, now located on west side of town. *Bentley Historical Library.*

Right: Bimbo's, a longtime favorite of townies. *Bentley Historical Library.*

Below: Bimbo's on the Hill. *Bentley Historical Library.*

Whiffletree, around 1973. *Bentley Historical Library.*

decor, pitchers of Faygo redpop and live music from a Dixieland jazz band, occasionally fronted by the owner, Matt "Bimbo" Chutich. People who crave Bimbo's recipe today can find it at other still-operating Bimbo's locations in Kalamazoo, Michigan, and Hibbing, Minnesota.

The Whiffletree was a restaurant on Huron Street owned by Robby Babcock and Andy Gulzevan. The Whiffletree was beloved for its signature salad dressing, which could sometimes be found at other restaurants founded by its owners if you knew to ask. In 1988, the Whiffletree's building on East Huron Street was heavily damaged by fire. Babcock and Gulzevan have separately opened a number of other restaurants since.

The Flaming Pit was a traditional American restaurant inside the Holiday Inn East on Washtenaw Avenue. It specialized in big steaks and stiff drinks and had quite a popular happy hour. Decorated in a colonial style, it also hosted live events like the Ypsilanti Dinner Theater and was a Saturday football destination in the 1970s. The Pit was succeeded in 1985 by Gollywobbler, a nautical-themed restaurant owned by the Whiffletree's Robby Babcock. In 1996, the space became Siam Square, which remains there today, now attached to the Victory Inn & Suites.

Flaming Pit, around 1971. *Bentley Historical Library.*

The Bombay Bicycle Club was located between Wolverine Tower and the Sheraton Hotel off of Boardwalk Drive. Though lore tells that it was part of a chain, the chain doesn't appear to have any national presence now. The restaurant closed in the 1990s, and the space became a location for Damon's, a ribs restaurant that boasted a then-unprecedented wall of projection screens for guests to watch enjoy multiple sports events at once. The Damon's chain eventually contracted; an independently owned location near Cincinnati is the closest to Ann Arbor today and still serves the ribs and the onion loaf. The space was empty for a year until its current tenant, Buffalo Wild Wings, opened in 2014.

Robert and Adeline Thompson opened DeLong's Bar-B-Q Pit in 1964 in a converted gas station across from the Kerrytown Farmers' Market. Its tangy sweet signature sauce was made in forty-four-gallon batches every month and tasted just as good on a side of fries as on a rack of ribs. As the Thompsons aged, their daughter, Diana McKnight Morton, took over operations at the restaurant; she retired and closed it in 2001. The space is now occupied by an Asian restaurant, Tesuya; legend tells that the Thompsons will still sell you a jar of the sauce.

Moveable Feast began as a bakery in Kerrytown, then was a table-service restaurant in a house at Liberty and Second Streets. In the 1990s, it returned to Kerrytown to open a café. In 1997, the Feast changed ownership, and its new owners retreated from Kerrytown again to concentrate on the Liberty Street house. In 2004, they exited the restaurant business but continue to cater and plan events.

The Bagel Factory's glass-and-metal building stood out among the apartments and the brick buildings of the neighboring Village Corner. Although the restaurant, on South University Avenue near Forest Avenue, offered deli sandwiches and breakfast options, its signature menu item was a fried sweet bagel called a fragel. Bagel Fragel, on Plymouth Road, still serves them, though it was searching for a new location on the north side of Ann Arbor as this book went to press.

Jesse Campbell was Mr. Rib, a beloved fixture of Ann Arbor from Main Street to Packard Street. Though he offered all manner of meats, Campbell's signature sandwich was the Soul on a Roll, combining smoked beef and pork, his own Jesse's Pride sauce and a generous portion of coleslaw. A 1960 graduate of Ann Arbor High, Campbell worked in the auto industry for a

The Bagel Factory. *Bentley Historical Library.*

decade before opening Barbeque King in 1974 at North Main and Summit Streets. After a failed partnership and a stint as a liquor-licensed party store, Campbell relaunched as Mr. Rib in the Main and Summit location in 1985. The original store closed in 1991, but Campbell continued to sell barbeque at Michigan football games and in the parking lot of Buster's Food Mart at Packard Street and Platt Road. Campbell also worked construction jobs to outfit a commissary near the Ann Arbor Airport and reopened at Packard Street and Carpenter Road in the spring of 1993. (This location was named one of "America's 10 Best Rib Joints" by *Car & Driver* magazine, whose offices were located nearby on Hogback Road.) Legend tells that Campbell's generosity made it difficult for him to keep up with rent, and the Packard and Carpenter location closed in the fall of 1994. In 1995, Mr. Rib reappeared on Packard Street near Platt Road again, this time in a restaurant space with indoor seating. This location was a good fit for the business and remained open for a few years. Even after the restaurant's closure, Mr. Rib continued to do great catering business and sold out of pop-up locations until Campbell passed away in 2006.

Maude's, described as "the secret garden of Ann Arbor restaurants," originally opened in 1977 when Dennis Serras, then a manager of the Real Seafood Company, and a partner purchased the Golden Falcon restaurant on Fourth Avenue, soon expanding into the neighboring Beckwith Evans carpet store. The original Maude's had a Gay Nineties bawdy house theme and offered sandwiches, salads and crab legs by the pound. In 1993, the owners updated the decor in a new American bistro style, and they pivoted again in 1996 into a classy barbeque joint. The 1996 change moved the restaurant's famous ribs out of the kitchen into an outdoor smoker, which some past employees blame for the restaurant's closure the following year. The owners tried a Mexican restaurant, Arriba, in the space. That lasted about a year and a half. In the years that followed, nightclub concepts were tested there but attracted police attention. Today, the building hosts a branch of the business-lunch staple Ruth's Chris Steak House.

The building that contains the storefronts of 118 and 120 West Liberty Street was built in part by Adam and Anton Schaeberle in the late 1860s. Originally, the shops housed the brothers' harness shop, the offices of the Ann Arbor Central Mills and a flour and feed shop owned by John Laubengeyer. Much later, Leo Ping's, which specialized in Cantonese food, called 118 home. The space later became an upscale eatery called Leopold Blooms, then Larry's Restaurant and then Trattoria Bongiovanni in 1983, and it soon found itself renamed Trattoria Bella Ciao around 1985. Since

Interior shot of Maude's. *Courtesy of Sam Misuraca.*

2009, local chef Brandon Johns has run his farm-to-table restaurant, the Grange. The storefronts next door at 120 were home to Andy's Bar and Mr. Flood's Party.

The Parthenon was a traditional Greek restaurant converted from a Cunningham Drugs. It remained at Liberty and Main Streets until the 2010s, when the owner retired and sold to Washington Street's popular Café Habana, which moved to the busy corner beneath a restaurant called Lena. The space is now occupied by the Pretzel Bell.

Thano's Lamplighter was a Greek restaurant and pizzeria at the intersection of Liberty and Thompson Streets, next door to Tally Hall/ Liberty Square. Thano's car could often be found parked in the adjacent alley, unmistakable with its "THANO" vanity plate.

Located at 109 South Main Street, the Preketes family's Sugar Bowl restaurant served patrons from 1911 until 1967. Originally from Greece, Paul Preketes came to the United States in 1903 and to Ann Arbor a year later. Paul and his brother Charles first opened a candy store at the 109–111 South Main Street location in 1911. Brothers Frank and Tony later joined the business as teenagers. During the 1930s, a University of Michigan student named Gerald Ford worked part-time at the restaurant.

The Round Table was a simple American restaurant with low prices and a dizzying array of pies. It was patronized for over fifty years, and one move,

Leo Ping's on West Liberty. *Bentley Historical Library.*

Sugar Bowl. *Bentley Historical Library.*

by a dedicated group of regulars who occupied the titular table. Originally named Freddy Haas, the restaurant on West Huron Street just east of Main Street began to cultivate this following in the early 1900s, when owner Haas began to offer a light lunch buffet with the purchase of alcohol. This special lasted fifteen years, and the crowd who came together for a free sandwich over a beer stayed together through Prohibition and beyond, through changes in ownership (first to Haas's assistant Dexter Davenport and finally to Willard Den Houter and employee Evelyn York Stack) and location: when the Ann Arbor Bank & Trust Company expanded its footprint and knocked down the Round Table's building in 1961, loyal customers followed the restaurant a year later to 114 West Liberty Street, where one of the big round tables was waiting for them. Evelyn continued to run the Round Table, living upstairs from the restaurant on Liberty Street, until 1993, when she retired to care for her aged mother and sold the restaurant to Andy Gulzevan, who owned Kitty O'Shea's next door. Both restaurants were run together for a while, Round Table for lunch and Kitty O'Shea's for dinner, until 1995, when the Kana Korean restaurant moved from the University of Michigan Medical Campus into the Round Table's space. (Kitty O'Shea's was closed at the same time, but was quickly reoccupied by the Flame Bar, which moved from its longtime Washington Street location.)

Oyster Bar & the Spaghetti Machine (known as OBSM) was owned by Greg Fenerli, an Ann Arbor entrepreneur who was previously known for the Rubaiyat Continental Dining Room, and was operated downstairs from the Rubaiyat (later Zorba's). Nearly its entire menu was summed up in its name. It served fresh raw oysters and house-made spaghetti with over a dozen different sauces. OBSM was beloved for its ingredients, many locally sourced. Patrons marveled at its stock of fresh tomatoes year-round. Robby Babcock of the Whiffletree and Gollywobbler acquired both Zorba's and OBSM in 1989. In 1995, Babcock sold OBSM and its upstairs neighbor, Robby's at the Icehouse, to Detroit-area restaurateur Al Balooly.

In 1965, the Bolgos Farms dairy expanded its retail store into a roadside attraction for U.S. 23 travelers just a few yards from the Plymouth Road exit. It sold Bolgos dairy products (bottled next door at 3601 Plymouth Road) and other grocery items at a convenience store in the back. The restaurant, with its distinctive round dining room and gull-wing carousel roof, served a full menu. In 1967, Bolgos opened another dining room with a German buffet downstairs from the main restaurant. This was known as the Tuebingen Room, in honor of Ann Arbor's sister city in Germany. In 1976, the Bolgos family sold their trucks and equipment to Twin Pines Dairy of Detroit and redeveloped the farmland. A Red Roof Inn was built on the site of the plant and stands to this day. The Bolgos Restaurant reopened in 1979 as the first Ann Arbor location for Forbidden City Chinese restaurant, though its corner plot is now a CVS Pharmacy.

The Rubaiyat Continental Dining Room opened in the Curtis Building (341 South Main Street) in 1960 as a sophisticated restaurant with three dining rooms and liquor served by the glass (the first public establishment to do so in Ann Arbor). It expanded in 1961 and again in 1965—much of the construction was performed by the restaurant's owner, Greg Fenerli, an immigrant and Michigan engineering alum. In 1970, the restaurant moved to the corner of Huron and First Streets. (Until Rubaiyat moved in, the building there had been a Saab auto dealer and before that an ice company; going forward, it would house restaurants and bars.) This incarnation of the Rubaiyat included a dinner theater, though by the mid-1970s, the food menu would be history and the dinner theater would give way to DJs and disco music. Until the Nectarine Ballroom arrived on the scene, the Rubaiyat was the only disco in town and one of only a few hangouts for gay people. In 1986, Fenerli abruptly closed the Rubaiyat and relaunched it a couple of months later as Zorba's, a Greek restaurant, which he operated alongside Oyster Bar & the Spaghetti Machine in the same building.

Just prior to its 1971 debut, the alternative Ann Arbor *Sun* newspaper declared Indian Summer "an outrageous improvement on what used to be the Virginian Restaurant." A vegetarian, natural-foods restaurant, it sourced its produce from Nettle's Farm in Stockbridge and its bread from the local nonprofit Harmony Bakery. Tempura was the restaurant's signature item, though it was also well regarded for house-made salad dressings and fresh fruit dishes. Indian Summer was a partner, along with other food co-ops and restaurants, in the Tribal Council Food Committee, a nonprofit concession that served music festivals and other events in town. In 1976, Indian Summer was replaced by Govinda's, an Indian vegetarian restaurant.

The original Metzger's German American Restaurant was opened by the Metzger and Kuhn families in 1928. Wilhelm and Marie Metzger and their children, along with their partner Christian Kuhn, rented the space from the Flautz family and named their original restaurant the German American. Metzger's restaurant resided in the Ashley Street–Washington Street location until 1936, when it moved to Fourth Avenue and Washington Street. In 1946, Wilhelm's brother Fritz Metzger bought the Old German Restaurant next door. Today, the third and fourth generations of Metzgers, including John Metzger, continue the tradition of excellent service and delicious German

Old German in 1977. *Bentley Historical Library.*

food at the Metzger's restaurant in nearby Scio Township. Meanwhile, a new version of the Old German Restaurant opened on Washington Street in 2013. The new bar, while unaffiliated with the Metzger family, features an Old German sign as well as a table from the original restaurant.

Bicycle Jim's was a popular bar on campus upstairs at South University Avenue and Forest Street. It was later rebranded as Cactus Jack's and then Mitch's Place. As rents began to take off in the early 2000s, it moved to a smaller location above the Princeton Review, kitty-corner on Forest Street. That location finally closed in 2010.

San Fu, at South Main Market, was beloved for dependably good Chinese takeout. The family who owned it retired when the South Main Market site was purchased and razed to erect the Yard student apartment complex.

Mark's Carts was founded in 2011 by Mark Hodesh in an alley behind his Downtown Home and Garden store. It was the first Ann Arbor space to welcome food trucks, with a changing lineup every season from spring to late autumn. It served as both an opportunity for restaurants from outside downtown to offer their food to downtown workers (Satchel's BBQ, Hut-K Cha'ats) and as an incubator for great ideas to make the leap to permanent spaces (the Lunch Room, Miss Kim). After selling Downtown Home and Garden to a loyal employee, Mark Hodesh continued to operate Mark's Carts for another year before closing the space in 2017.

Located at 605 East William Street between State and Maynard Streets and open late into the night during the 1960s and 1970s, Mark's Coffeehouse (no relations to Mark's Carts) served as a meeting place for countless students looking to play chess, drink coffee or just hang out. It remains known as the first bohemian coffeehouse in Ann Arbor. Nearby was the short-lived Promethean Coffee at 508 East William Street, which served Viennese-style coffee, spun jazz records and featured the occasional live folk music show.

During the 1960s and 1970s, the Cleveland-based chain of Amy Joy donuts had a store at 2030 West Stadium Boulevard. Housed in an A-frame building, the donut shop was one of the few places for a late-night bite. Today, Dimo's is at that address and uses some Amy Joy recipes for its donuts.

Not Another Café (NAC) was downstairs at South University and Forest Avenues in the 1990s. It succeeded Community Newscenter in a radical reimagining of the space. As a student-oriented restaurant, it stayed open very late—until 4:00 a.m. on the weekends. NAC served the usual coffeehouse fare with a limited hot food menu but also encouraged hanging out years before bars and other coffeehouses did, with board games and a stage for live music and a glassed-in area for smokers. Matthew Chicoine performed DJ sets here before achieving international fame as Recloose.

Eve Aronoff, who achieved national fame as a contestant on *Top Chef*, owned eve, the restaurant. After years in various roles in the restaurant industry, Aronoff opened eve in Kerrytown in 2003. Diners loved the intimate location inside Kerrytown, though its lack of a prep kitchen made running dinners a labor-intensive process, especially after Aronoff's appearance on season six of *Top Chef*, a TV competition series for professional chefs. In the wake of her *Top Chef* publicity, Aronoff opened her second restaurant, Frita Batidos, a fast-casual Cuban-inspired hamburger spot. As Zingerman's sought out a temporary production space near its flagship deli, the restaurant closed in Kerrytown in 2011. In 2015, eve reopened inside the Bell Tower Hotel on Thayer Street. The macadamia-encrusted salmon was back alongside new dishes inspired by the seasons and more vegetarian options. Aronoff closed this location after a couple of years, citing water damage to the space. Aronoff helped to open, and designed the menu for, Dessous, an Indian/French fusion restaurant on Main Street, in 2018. Meanwhile, Frita Batidos periodically hosts special events with an eve-inspired menu.

Other Restaurant Memories

Many, many restaurants have graced the streets of Ann Arbor. This list is not exhaustive but hopefully will bring back some happy memories of first dates, tasty treats and solid meals: Eastern Accents (Fourth Avenue), Lovin' Spoonful (Main Street ice cream parlor), 328 South Main (now home of Prickly Pear), A&W Drive-In, Great Lakes Steak Company (State Street), Cloverleaf Dairy (where Northside Grill is now), Curtis Chicken in the Rough (South Main Street), Red Bull (Hogback Road), Grand Traverse Pie Company, the Apartment Lounge (near the Veterans Administration hospital), Arriba (Mexican restaurant where Maude's was), the Athenian, Bacchus Garden (where Ashley's is now), Bella Ciao (West Liberty Street), Betsy Ross (near Nickels Arcade), Bev's Caribbean Kitchen (Packard Street and Woodlawn Avenue), Forbidden City (3535 Plymouth Road), Gianelli's Pizza, Hinodae (State Street), Cherry Blossom (South State Street), Cracked Crab (where Café Zola is), Miller's Ice Cream (one on South University Avenue and one on Main Street), La Pinata (Stadium Boulevard and Liberty Street), Central Café (South Main Street), D'Amato's (102 South First Street), Dinersty (Liberty Street), Escoffier (Thayer Street), Everett's Drive-in (2280 West Stadium Boulevard), Flim Flam (Plymouth Road Mall), Jefferson Market (gourmet lunch/dinner counter at the market on Jefferson Street), Joe Joe's (North Fourth Avenue), Kav's Café (Kerrytown), Fowler's Pancake House (Stadium Boulevard and Liberty Street), Shehan-Shah (Washington Street), La Zamaan, Leo Ping's (South State Street near Hill Street), Loma Linda (Broadway Street), Mahek (East Washington Street), Manikas (South Main Street), Sweet Lorraine's (near Farmers Market), Middle Kingdom, Roy's Squeeze-in (Detroit Street), Shalimar (Washington Street), Seoul Korner (William and Thompson Streets), Taqueria La Tica (Packard Street and Woodlawn Avenue), Gino's (State and Washington Streets, replaced by Olga's), Mysore Woodlands (where Delong's was located), La Seine (Main Street where Sugar Bowl was), Swede's Diner (Fifth Avenue), Squares Restaurant (Liberty Street where Dinersty was), What Crepe, Wafel Shop, Manika's Sirloin House (South Main Street), Stadium Restaurant (where Ashley's is now), Sze-Chuan West (West Stadium Boulevard), Thompson's Restaurant (215 North Main Street), Yamato (Kerrytown), Zanzibar (South State Street), Zenaida Chocolate Lounge (South Main Street), Zydeco (Main Street), Steve's Lunch (South University Avenue), Pita Pit, Pizza Pino (now Satchel's downtown), @burger (now Tomukun), Five Guys downtown (located on State Street after Shaman Drum closed, now Piada) and the Earl of Sandwich chain on State Street.

Even some of our fast-food chain restaurants provided some interesting times. The McDonald's on Maynard Street was said to be the first with a second floor (the upstairs was a continuation of the dining room). It closed in the 1990s to make way for a new building that now contains the Aveda Institute as well as University of Michigan offices. There was also a location on South University Avenue where Bubble Island is now. This location was athletics-themed, with Michigan decorations and memorabilia (similar to the Stadium Boulevard McDonald's now). It had a block-M-shaped island in the middle of the dining area with plants and counters to sit at. Burger King could be found below street level on the southwest corner of Maynard and Liberty Streets and on South University Avenue where Starbucks is now. A chain that began in the Detroit area, Little Caesars, was on South University Avenue where Blue Leprechaun is now and in the basement of the Michigan Union where Ahmo's is now. Years before the Little Caesars chain pivoted to the inexpensive "Hot & Ready" model, this store did a three-dollar medium, ninety-nine-cent crazy bread special on Wednesday nights that filled the basement of the union every week.

In the 1980s and 1990s, a Taco Bell was located on South University Avenue, where it was open all day but really catered to students and the party crowd. Without the drive-through window that most late-night fast-food joints depend on, it was forced to maintain its dining room late into the evening as well as the mischief that attracted. When Taco Bell closed, its space eventually became Mia Za, a fast-casual Italian restaurant primarily located in Big Ten cities. Taco Bell would eventually return to the Michigan League Underground, a dining area on campus. Although popular at lunch, the building's limited hours and lack of a drive-through window prevented it from capturing the late crowd, and Taco Bell left the area once again in 2014.

3
HOSPITALITY AND RECREATION

Be Our Guest and Have a Great Time While You're Here!

Ann Arbor prides itself on its welcoming and affirming nature. Year after year, we consistently rank among the best places to live in the United States. When you visit today, you can enjoy award-winning restaurants, world-class theater and music venues and comfortable hotels, and it seems it was that way from the start.

Ann Arbor's hospitality industry officially started with the Washtenaw Coffee House. When people came to the newly settled town and needed a place to stay, they went to the home of Elisha and Mary Ann Rumsey at First Avenue and Huron Street. But as more and more folks arrived, Ann Arbor needed additional lodgings.

In 1832, William R. Thomson opened the Washtenaw House Hotel on Broadway in Lower Town. Inside the three-story building was a bar and ballroom. Not much information about the hotel remains today, but our first governor was a guest there, and in its day, the inn was known as the finest between Chicago and Detroit. By 1857, Washtenaw House had a new proprietor by the name of W.W. Wells. He and his wife, Diana, had two children, and he was described as a "courteous landlord." The building was torn down in 1927.

Many hotels surrounded the Courthouse Square back in the day. Our first large hotel was the Franklin House, located at the northwest corner of Main and Huron Streets, the former site of John Allen's log blockhouse. Across the way at Huron Street and Fourth Avenue

Camp Hee-Haw orchestra, around 1908. *Bentley Historical Library.*

sat Cook's Hotel, later renamed Cook's Temperance House. Owners Anna and Solon Cook were teetotalers and eschewed any alcohol on the premises—a wooden staircase at the residential lofts across the street still shows evidence of kegs being dragged up and down the steps, as guests of the temperance hotel crossed the street for their beer during the Cooks' ownership, which lasted until after the Civil War. In 1871, new owners replaced the old wooden hotel with a modern brick building. A 1910 fire led to further remodeling and a new name, the Allenel—a mix of founder John Allen's name and the word "hotel." Like many hotels of its day, the Allenel boasted a fancy dining room and a bar. Common knowledge, however, dictated that guests avoid rooms above the second floor, as the place was such a fire trap that one wanted the ability to jump to safety should the need arise. Former first lady Betty Ford spent her honeymoon night at the hotel and attested to the fact that she refused to go any higher than floor two; former president Gerald Ford said in his autobiography that he "paid for that night a thousand times." In 1967, a Sheraton Inn replaced the Allenel, later renamed the Ann Arbor Inn. In 1990, the hotel shut its doors, and the building was converted into what

The Allenel Hotel was known as the best hotel in town. *Bentley Historical Library.*

is now the Courthouse Square apartments for seniors, with the Blom Meadworks on the first floor.

The west side had its own place to stay, eat and drink. The Germania Hotel, located where the Earle and Sweetwaters currently sit at the southeast corner of Washington and Ashley Streets, had more than just hotel rooms. Built by Michael Staebler, the building hosted meetings of the Germania Society, dances, balls and lectures. In 1895, the family renamed it the American Hotel and added a fourth floor. An 1891 advertisement boasted modern refits and steam heating throughout for just two dollars per day. Around the same time, lodgers could find a slightly less expensive place to

The elegant American Hotel dining room. *Bentley Historical Library.*

American Hotel at 123 West Washington Street, where the Earle and Sweetwaters are now located. *Bentley Historical Library.*

stay on West Huron Street where the St. James Hotel offered rooms for fifty cents cheaper.

Located at the southwest corner of Main and Ann Streets, the Hotel Whitney was next to the Whitney Theater. Stars who were touring the area usually stayed at the conveniently located hotel. This was also the original site for Hill's Opera House; today, it is a surface parking lot.

Though an evening in Ann Arbor's historic hotels may sound appealing, they also had a tendency to reflect the ignoble attitudes of the time. No advertisement actually says that African Americans were forbidden to grace the premises, and no articles about a "whites only" clientele were written. But interestingly, the Forester's Hotel, in what is now Kerrytown, was known as the hotel "under colored management." The Kayser Block also housed accommodations for African American residents and was known as a place to go for new arrivals.

As the decades marched on, more and more hotels sprang up. At the corner of Washtenaw Avenue and Huron Parkway sat the Arbor Lodge Motel. The Stage Stop Motel, located at 2443 Carpenter Road, featured a real stagecoach out front. Lower Town contained the University Motel

Whitney Theater, at the corner of Main and Ann Streets (now a surface lot). *Bentley Historical Library.*

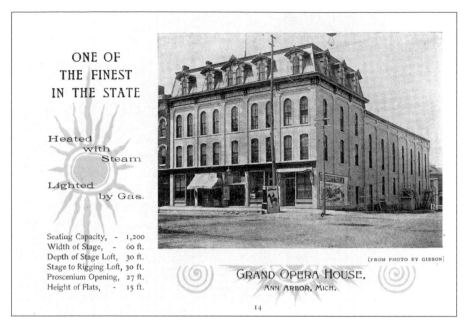

George D. Hill's Opera House. *Bentley Historical Library.*

at 1000 Broadway. The corner of Fourth Avenue and Huron Street in downtown was home to several hotels, including the Ann Arbor Inn, which burned in 1975. More recently, the Michigan Inn on Jackson Road was finally demolished after many years of legal issues.

CHARLES KEYSER AND THE KAYSER BUILDING

In 1899, Charles F. Kayser built a new three-story structure at 209–211 North Fourth Avenue. The original structure on that site was built by Samuel Sutherland and housed a gun shop, according to an *Argus-Democrat* article. Pictures of this original building are lost to history, but the structure was reported to have used bog lime and marl; the masons who built it were paid two dollars per day. Kayser's building was used as a hotel through World War I. City directories reported that managers were usually African American. In the early 1920s, the Colored Welfare League (CWL) purchased the building using proceeds from send-off parties thrown by local African American leaders, who felt that their recruits were

Kayser Building. *Bentley Historical Library.*

not getting the same elaborate send-offs as white recruits. This ownership was important, as it allowed the CWL to evict the Huron Club, known, according to *Historic Buildings, Ann Arbor, Michigan,* as a "local gambling den and house of prostitution." The CWL then turned the space into a community center for African Americans. At the time, the YMCA did not allow African American children to use its facilities, so this new service was much needed.

One of the first groups to utilize the repurposed building was the Dunbar Center. Named for poet Paul Laurence Dunbar, the group provided classes, social and education programs and dances. In 1926, the Dunbar Center moved to 1009 East Catherine Street and, eleven years later, to 420 North Fourth Avenue. It eventually morphed into the Ann Arbor Community Center on North Main Street, which was recently sold to a tech firm. In addition to members of the Dunbar Center, many other fraternal organizations rented space on the second floor—the Black Elks, St. Mary's Lodge, the Household of Ruth Lodge and Eastern Star. On Thursday evenings in the 1930s, a group of women met to socialize, and men who worked for white fraternities at the University of Michigan also met there.

During these early years, the second floor of the Kayser Building housed University of Michigan School of Law graduate, active NAACP member and WCL attorney John Ragland. By the 1930s, a barbershop and beauty salon made their home on the ground floor. Owned by Samuel Elliot and Olive Lowery, respectively, these businesses catered to an African American clientele. A tearoom first named Josephine's Tea Room and later Julia's Tea Room (to reflect a change in owners) operated from 1937 to 1943. In addition to serving food and drinks, the restaurant also held the occasional séance fundraiser. After the business closed, the second floor was converted into apartments.

A young African American barber named J.D. Hall purchased the building in 1966. His barbershop occupied the space on the north part of the building. For most of the 1980s, the Danish News operated out of the building until the "red light district" was officially shut down. In 1989, Fourth Avenue Birkenstock opened in the space to the left of the barbershop. During Hall's ownership, groups such as Model Cities, the Women's Crisis Center and the Community Leaning Post rented space on the second floor, while the third floor remained as rented rooms.

But what of Charles Kayser? He lived a long and seemingly pleasant life. He was born in the city in 1863 and passed away at his home on 322 East Ann Street eighty-six years later. He manufactured cigars at his shop in the 100 block of North Main Street and was a member of the Elks and the Bethlehem Church. He and his wife, Anna, did not have children. He was laid to rest in Forest Hill Cemetery.

CELEBRATIONS AND RECREATION

Arcades

Just as it did in many other cities, the arcade craze hit Ann Arbor. Double Focus was located at Packard and State Streets in an area that sees frequent turnover in businesses (Craft Breww City is there now). In the same area, the building now housing a revamped Blue Front was briefly home to an arcade. Simulation Station was located on Liberty Street between Maynard and Thompson Streets. Part of a Detroit-area chain of arcades, it featured coin-operated games as well as a motion simulator ride called the Amazin' Blue Machine. Another chain, Chuck E. Cheese, could be found at Liberty Street and Stadium Boulevard in a bright-pink castle. Over in the Michigan Union, students could take a break at the Study Break arcade in the basement or head to South University and Forest Avenues to play at the Great Escape. On the southeast side of town, gamers of all ages could play at Aladdin's Castle inside Arborland Mall or head a little west to Briarwood Mall, which featured a Fun Factory franchise. Other arcades included Mickey Rats and Focus Pinball.

Argo Beach

In the early part of the twentieth century, the city of Ann Arbor had a municipal beach at what is now the Argo canoe launch. Argo Dam was purchased by Detroit Edison in 1905. Twelve years later, the company offered to build a beach if the city would agree to maintain it. After it reached an agreement with the city, Detroit Edison brought in the sand necessary for a beach and even built a pier and docks. For two decades, the city paid one dollar a year to rent the property; it bought the beach in 1938.

The beach was not the only attraction. Paul Tessmer owned a boathouse on the North Main Street side of Argo Pond, west of the pond. Tessmer built over one hundred canoes, renting them along with rowboats to patrons. At some point, the facility was moved across the pond near the beach. By that time, William Saunders owned and operated the boathouse, selling snacks to hungry swimmers from the canoe livery.

This bygone era did not have the same environmental regulations that we have today. Nevertheless, the city did make improvements to the beach in 1936. In the early 1940s, city council questioned the water quality, and the beach closed in 1948.

Swimming pool at Fifth Avenue and Hill Street. *Bentley Historical Library.*

For more swimming opportunities, residents could head to Weinberg's coliseum and swimming pool at Fifth Avenue and Hill Street, which provided fun for local children and adults for years. Inside the building was the city's first indoor ice rink, which was home to the University of Michigan hockey team until 1973. Roller skaters used the balcony for their sport, and everyone enjoyed the sounds of the Wurlitzer player organ. The outside rink was over a decade older but served its purpose well—and doubled as a swimming pool in warmer months. Fresh springs from a nearby property fed water to the pool. When it was too cold to swim but too warm for ice, the coliseum hosted speeches, circuses, horse shows, dances and other indoor festivals.

Holidays and Celebrations in Old Ann Arbor

In July 1824, Ann Arbor was home to only a handful of pioneer families, but that didn't stop them from celebrating Independence Day. The Woodruff family, settlers of the future Ypsilanti, invited the whole county to honor the birthday of our country. Benjamin Woodruff Jr. recited the Declaration of Independence, everyone sang "Hail Columbia," and then they all enjoyed a hearty feast prepared by Mrs. Freelove Woodruff. By the next year, Ann Arbor was ready to celebrate on its own. Elisha Rumsey gathered the small military company for a march from the Courthouse Square to the oak grove where St. Andrew's Church now stands. Over three hundred people gathered to watch the parade, and many then dined at John Allen's residence.

One of the biggest celebrations was German American Day. In 1891, Paul G. Suckey of Manchester explained that October 6, 1683, was the day when Germans first landed in "greater numbers on the hospitable shores of our new fatherland." He touted the hard work of the poor laborers (mostly weavers), who toiled to ensure acceptance in their new land and to make a new and better life for themselves and their families. Likewise, Suckey said, those living in Washtenaw County were working hard to do the same.

The festival served to commemorate these successes in a way different from celebrations of other nationalities yet still be "distinctively American in every respect." The event rotated amongst various communities in the county, and in 1896, Ann Arbor hosted the party. After the downtown parade, revelers went to a huge picnic at Relief Park on Madison Street to continue the celebration.

The May Festival began in 1894 and featured three concerts over a two-day period. Presented by the University Musical Society, the event doubled in size by 1919. It lasted until May 1995.

The opening of a new civic venture was also reason for a party. In 1897, the Germania Hall opened at the corner of Second and William Streets. A grand "Festball" was held, featuring a warm welcome from Mayor Charles Hiscock and a performance by the Ann Arbor Orchestra. The social hall went on to host many other events during its existence.

Civic organizations celebrated their anniversaries in style. In 1897, the Independent Order of Odd Fellows honored its seventy-eighth birthday with a daylong party featuring music, speakers and a catered dinner. Only one "lady speaker" was featured; Emma E. Bower made "many sly digs" at her brothers in the order and managed not to impugn the "reputation of the fair sex as speakers," according to the *Argus* newspaper.

Amending the Constitution provided reason for celebration in 1870. The adoption of the Fifteenth Amendment led to a two-day celebration in our town. Bands from Ypsilanti and Detroit met and marched through downtown and then to the courthouse, where former governor Alpheus

Women enjoy a ride at 331 East Ann Street in the 1920s. *Bentley Historical Library.*

Felch and others made speeches. Dinner and dancing then commenced at the Good Templars' Hall.

Dancing parties were everywhere. In 1897, an "inspection hop" was announced. After the annual inspection of the armory, everyone was invited to come on down and dance. Dancing parties could frequently be found at Granger's Dancing Hall on Maynard Street near Liberty Street or on the third floor at Hangsterfer's on the southwest corner of Main and Washington Streets.

Additionally, residents held many events in private homes. Box socials were popular at the end of the nineteenth century. At these parties, women would decorate a box, fill it with lunch or dinner for two and then put the box up for bidding. The winning man would then join the lady for a meal. Since the boxes did not have the woman's name on it, anyone could end up with anyone. The social raised money for various good causes, such as the one in 1899 that raised sixty-five dollars for a school library. Garden parties, "at homes" and wedding celebrations were also held in private homes.

Parades

Parades have been a part of life in Ann Arbor since its earliest days. In 1861, the *Michigan Argus* honored the soldiers of Camp Fountain with a public dinner and parade. The paper reported that despite the look of the sky, farmers and their families flooded in with enough "substantials and luxuries [to] satisfy and delight the physical man." In 1897, the Ann Arbor Cycle Club had a "monster bicycle parade" accompanied by buglers. Their purpose was to have fun but also to demonstrate the large number of bicycles in the city and the need for good roads to ride upon.

In 1883, the biggest day of the year in Ann Arbor (according to the *Courier*, anyway) was the day when the circus came to town from Lansing. Of particular interest was the "mastodon," Jumbo, who ate up all the candy and peanuts in town. In 1897, the Barnum and Bailey Company based its parade around a re-creation of Columbus's return to Barcelona after his discoveries in the New World. The *Ann Arbor Argus* promised wild beasts, golden chariots, hippodrome riders and a team of forty horses driven by one man. The 1898 Ringling Brothers circus parade featured elephant comedians, a traveling aviary and, of course, acrobats.

While most of these parades happened in fairer weather, Ann Arbor did see a midwinter circus announced via a parade including the Light Infantry

Parade down Main Street. *Bentley Historical Library.*

and local city bands. This circus, according to the newspaper, "must be seen by everybody who enjoys a good laugh."

After the turn of the century, circus parades continued to delight. The Parker & Watts parade brought the usual elephants and floats to town in the 1930s. But other events were honored and celebrated as well. In 1918, the city held an Armistice Day parade. During World War II, the parades took on a patriotic air. There were several war bond parades, as well as a 1943 parade featuring a Japanese submarine. After the death of President Roosevelt, the University of Michigan Soldiers led a parade in his honor.

There were also parades to raise money for polio research. Groups like the American Legion Drum and Bugle Corps participated in these events to raise money for the March of Dimes.

During happier times, Christmas parades brought Santa to town. The jolly old elf brought along his reindeer in a spirited parade down Main Street. Ever the kind-hearted soul, Santa then visited children who were hospitalized. The Michigan Eagles hosted a parade of drill teams and performers to close their conventions. In the spring, there was a Michigras

Parade down Main Street. *Bentley Historical Library.*

The post office and court lawn as a parade goes by. *Bentley Historical Library.*

Parade with float made of apples. *Bentley Historical Library.*

parade to go along with the Michigras celebration at the university. This event united town and gown with extravagant floats and much fun.

Every October saw numerous school costume parades around the neighborhoods. The chamber of commerce also put on a Halloween parade featuring not just costumed revelers but also clowns, floats and marching bands. November saw the Veterans' Day parade, featuring uniformed veterans from all areas of service. Even the Soap Box Derby was reason enough for a parade featuring marchers, dancers and a queen. And of course, the University of Michigan hosted annual homecoming parades filled with floats, bands and the homecoming queen.

Fireworks

In 1956, Nathan Kelsay, the owner of Kelsay's Super Market, saw a fireworks display in Ypsilanti. He decided that Ann Arbor should enjoy such a spectacular show and worked with area businesspeople to make it so. The men started a group called the Spirit of '76 Club and put on a show at Buhr Park. This group continued until 1969, when the Ann Arbor Jaycees took over the festivities. Ten years later, the show moved to the airport, which hosted fireworks for the Fourth of July until insurance costs forced the city to end the event in 1991.

SPORTS AND RECREATION

Debating Club

Ann Arbor managed to make its own fun in its early days. As early as 1840, we had a debating club. According to the many ads placed in our newspapers, the club met on Saturdays at Ormsby's Block. While it appears that only men debated, the ads did mention that "ladies and gentlemen are respectfully invited to attend." Teams of two or four argued for or against resolutions that included that "the works of nature are more pleasing to the eye than the works of art," "money begets more friends than talent," "lawyers are indispensably necessary to the peace and harmony of society" and "labor saving machinery is beneficial to the laboring classes."

Bowling

Ann Arborites seem to really have enjoyed bowling for sport and exercise. As far back as the 1880s, our citizens engaged in the game. Ads in the Ann Arbor *Courier* touted bowling as helping one's circulation, digestion and appetite. Bliss' Bowling Alley put its money where its ad was by offering a contest for those making the most points in twenty-five games between December and January. First prize was a ten-dollar medal, second prize was a box of cigars, and third prize was one dollar's worth of bowling tickets. A.C. Bliss & Company encouraged folks to come to its newly spruced up place, decorated in "good style" and located across from the courthouse. In January 1885, it was temporarily hampered by a fire caused by a burning chimney. Fortunately, the damage was limited to the paper on the wall near the chimney. Despite the minor damages, the *Courier* reported in April that the bowling alley had been moved to Turner Park. The park, located on West Madison Street between Fourth and Fifth Streets, had a bowling alley prior to February 11, 1885, but its roof caved in that February due to heavy snow. (While the park is gone, there is a Turner Park Court near this location.)

Bowling alleys were also found in other organizations. In April 1891, the *Ann Arbor Argus* reported that the YMCA's new board of directors proposed building a clubhouse. Estimated to cost around $10,000, the facility would include a bowling alley along with a billiards room, card room and smoking room. The hope was that the city's young men could spend their evenings in a place of "pleasant surroundings, with elevating influences."

McMillan Hall also had its own bowling alley, reported the *Ann Arbor Argus* in December 1891. The double bowling alley was scheduled to open in February 1893 with a one-dollar fee to use it; the expectation was that two hundred dollars would be raised. The paper reported that it was hoped that ladies would buy fifty of those two hundred tickets, as they would be allowed to use the gymnasium one fourth of the time it was open.

Located at the corner of Huron and State Streets and, according to the *Ann Arbor Argus*, "equally distant from the university and the business part of the city," Hobart Hall boasted its own fourteen-foot-by-seventy-foot bowling alley. There was also a Hobart Guild comprising male and female students connected with St. Andrew's Episcopal Church. Its clubhouse in Harris Hall included parlors for music and literary entertainment, a kitchen and dining room, bathrooms, billiard rooms and a bowling alley. A member could bowl for free but had to pay extra for billiards and bathrooms.

The bowling alley at the Michigan Union stood empty in this picture. Maybe bowlers were at the numerous other bowling alleys located around town? *Bentley Historical Library.*

The good times came to a bit of a halt in 1898, when common council passed an ordinance requiring bowling alleys and billiard halls to pay for a yearly five-dollar license and to close at 10:30 p.m. Alderman Henry Richards thought this was an "injustice" to the bowling alleys and that Ann Arbor should allow more of these types of business, as the proprietors paid taxes and rent. Conversely, Alderman John Koch opined that bowling alleys made too much noise, and Alderman Alonzo Stevens thought the five-dollar license was too small a price to pay. The *Ann Arbor Argus-Democrat* reported that because of this ordinance, a man who "handles one of those seductive wooden balls after the witching hour of 10:30 standard time will be breaking the laws of the municipality" and expressed irritation at how the council was "regulating the amusement of the people."

Despite these new restrictions, Ann Arborites kept bowling, and love for bowling continued into the twentieth century. In 1952, Huron Lanes opened at 316–320 East Huron Street. The sixteen-lane alley featured then-state-of-the-art technologies such as Tel-E-Score equipment that projected score sheets on large screens. Another innovation was the automatic ball return, which could also be adapted to allow people to practice bowling with no pins to perfect their delivery. The business added a restaurant in 1962 but was sold in 1967 and later demolished. Also in 1967, the Ann Arbor Recreation bowling alley at 605 East Huron Street was demolished to make room for the Campus Inn.

Concerts

The *Ann Arbor News* reported that our first rock concerts were held in West Park and drew upward of a thousand young people "and almost as many critics." Groups such as the Free Community Coalition and the Tribal Council advocated for free concerts to provide entertainment for younger crowds; however, there were concerns about drug use and traffic. (The *News* pointed out that many misconceptions about the concerts were made by people who never actually attended.) So in 1969, the promoters Trans Love Energies moved to less populated areas such as Gallup Park and Fuller

The Ark when it was at 1421 Hill Street. Since 1965, the Ark has entertained Ann Arbor with live performances almost every night of the year. Its first location was at 1421 Hill Street in a house built in 1894 by Michigan professor Henry Carter Adams. It then moved to 637½ Main Street and now resides at 316 South Main Street, still welcoming local and nationally known artists to the stage. *Bentley Historical Library.*

Left: Shakey Jake and friend dancing at a free concert. *Bentley Historical Library.*

Below, left to right: Linda, Anya and David Siglin on the steps of the Ark, 1978. In January 1969, David Siglin began working as the manager of the Ark, a position he held until 2008. He and his wife, Linda, worked tirelessly to turn the Ark into one of the most respected and beloved live music clubs in the country. This picture shows the Siglins and their daughter Anya on the steps of 1421 Hill Street. Anya is currently the Ark's program director. *Bentley Historical Library.*

Woman dancing at concert. *Bentley Historical Library.*

Road, and the criticism decreased. To handle the "hot and dirty work," a group called the Psychedelic Rangers was formed. These folks, who ranged in age from their mid-teens to their mid-twenties, were responsible for crowd control, parking issues and drug use prevention. It was made very clear that drug pushers would be not be allowed at the free concerts—they were told from the stage to leave and not return.

While the concerns about drugs and parking were dealt with, new problems arose. City budget problems almost killed the free concert series; fortunately, the Community Parks Program launched a massive fundraiser to save the shows. Their efforts included bucket drives, radio marathons, flea markets and benefit concerts. Thanks to their work, the concerts continued and drew upwards of five thousand people by the early 1970s.

Countless concerts have been held in Ann Arbor, but perhaps the most famous was the John Sinclair Freedom Rally. Held at Crisler Arena on December 10, 1971, the concert was a response to the ten-year prison sentence that writer and activist John Sinclair received for possessing two marijuana cigarettes. Performers included John Lennon, Yoko Ono, Phil Ochs, Bob Seger, Stevie Wonder and Commander Cody and His Lost Planet Airmen. Sinclair was released shortly after the rally.

Ice Skating

Ann Arborites have probably been ice skating since someone realized that the Huron River froze in the most delightful ways. (We also enjoyed roller skating—the first rink opened in 1884 at Ashley and Huron Streets). One of the earliest local mentions of ice skating comes from the *Michigan Argus*, which reprinted an article proclaiming skating as "one of the most exhilarating of all pastimes." It also recommended that one wear a "vail" in cold weather lest one catch the deadly disease of pneumonia and advised against carrying

Ice skating party on frozen Huron River. *Bentley Historical Library.*

anything in one's mouth while ice skating because, well, even in 1862 they knew that was not a wise thing to do.

The December 1, 1893 issue of the *Ann Arbor Argus* noted that over two hundred ice skaters were on the Huron River the previous Sunday. It also reported that skaters found Allmendinger's carp pond safe to skate on, if a "bit crowded." And the ice on the Argo Dam was "like an immense field of glass" as skaters flocked to it.

Pictures of happy kids skating at Burns or Allmendinger Park in the 1940s, 1950s and 1960s are easily found in the online archives of the *Ann Arbor News*. In 1964, the supervisor of the parks department, Sheldon Sproull, asked voters to approve a bond to pay for an outdoor artificial ice rink at Veterans Memorial Park. He noted that natural ice rinks were costly and difficult to maintain and that, if this rink was built, "the city possibly may find it can eliminate some of its 'natural' ice skating surfaces." The city built that ice rink at Veterans Park in 1972 and later another ice arena at Buhr Park. Thanks to the work of some former city council people, rinks are up at parks today for kids of all ages to enjoy.

MEDIA

Written Word

Back before the days of the internet, cable news and even radio, there was really only one place to get the lowdown on what was happening in your community: newspapers. And back in the 1800s and early 1900s, Ann Arborites had plenty of papers to choose from.

During the early era of newspapers, there was little pretense of being unbiased or neutral—a paper was Democratic, Republican, Whig, etc., and everyone knew which paper leaned toward which party. In 1829, Thomas Simpson began publishing the *Western Emigrant*. It was considered a "neutral" newspaper in that it leaned toward no political party. The paper advertised the young town to prospective settlers and kept current residents apprised of events in the outside world. Knowing that many newcomers were unable to bring their books with them, the *Western Emigrant* sought to offer "literary recreation, mental and moral improvement" to its readers as well as influence their political opinion.

Town cofounder John Allen backed the *Western Emigrant* and helped with editorial duties. In 1830, the paper relaunched as the *Emigrant*, edited by

Samuel Dexter, and carried a decidedly anti-Mason slant. (This bias was echoed in papers throughout the country. A New York man named William Morgan claimed that he was going to publish the secret of the Masons to the general public; when he disappeared later that same year, the Masons were blamed. Men around the country renounced their membership and publicly distanced themselves from all things Masonic.)

During the *Emigrant's* publication, locals could receive a year's subscription for $3.00 if paid in advance, $3.50 if paid at the end of the year. If someone could not pay money for delivery, produce would be accepted. At one point, no fewer than eight local agents dispatched the paper in neighboring towns. Judge Dexter continued this paper as the *Michigan Emigrant* in late 1830 and carried on until November 1834, when the paper ceased operations. Notable gems of the paper included a correspondent from Washington who sent his letters to John Allen; an advertisement for a "framed bridge over the Huron River" in the 1830s; and it was the first newspaper to advance the idea of a transcontinental railroad.

During the same period as the *Emigrant*, George Corselius published the *Michigan Whig*, whose title was a clue to which political party it favored. He published this paper for only about four months before rechristening it the *Michigan Whig and Washtenaw Democrat*.

In early 1835, E.P. Gardiner began publishing the *Michigan Argus*. Four years later, this paper continued on as the *Democratic Herald*—again, the very title suggesting which political party it favored. (Gardiner also published a paper called the *Morning Chronicle* but only produced one issue.) The *Democratic Herald* ran until 1842, when it was bought by E.R. Powell and Orrin Arnold; at some point, the owners rechristened it *True Democrat*.

The Michigan Anti-Slavery Society, under the auspices of Guy Beckley and Theodore Foster, began publishing the *Signal of Liberty* in 1841. During its publication, this nationally recognized paper publicized the horrors of human bondage and argued for the abolition of slavery. Beckley served as a Methodist minister, and his home on Pontiac Trail was a stop on the Underground Railroad. This well-known paper was not the first antislavery paper in Michigan, as that honor belonged to the *Michigan Freeman*, based out of Jackson. But while the *Freeman* only published sporadically, the *Signal* published almost every week. Josiah Beckley, brother of Guy, let his shop on Broadway serve as the print office and occasionally helped edit the journal.

The goal of the *Signal* was to influence the hearts and minds of citizens all over the country to take up the abolitionist mantle. To achieve this end, the publishers interviewed men and women who were emancipated and

Signal of Liberty newspaper. *Bentley Historical Library.*

published heartbreaking stories of slaves who were helpless as they watched family members get beaten and sold. They featured stories about free blacks in Michigan and elsewhere being lured away from their homes under false pretenses and sold into bondage. By incorporating national news with local information, Beckley and Foster succeeded in spreading the word about the horrific nature of slavery. They are credited with increasing the number of abolitionist groups and for helping to sway public opinion against the practice of owning human beings. The paper dissolved in 1847, but the cause was carried on by the *Michigan Liberty Press* in Battle Creek.

The *Michigan Times* published from 1837 until 1840 and was Democratic. Around that same time, the partnership of Seaman and L.W. Cole published the *Ann Arbor Journal* from 1838 until 1847, at which time it was continued as the *Washtenaw Whig*.

In 1846, the aforementioned L.W. Cole and E.P. Gardiner teamed up and began publishing a paper they called the *Michigan Argus* (it is not known

L.W. Cole and his *Argus* staff. *Bentley Historical Library.*

if this was in homage to his prior paper or if he just liked the name). The oldest known daguerreotype in Ann Arbor features Cole and his *Argus* staff in 1850.

The paper, which favored Democrats, became the *Weekly Michigan Argus* in 1854. On January 5, 1855, Elihu Pond took over the paper, sometimes including the word "Weekly" in the title, sometimes not. In 1879, the paper carried on as the *Ann Arbor Argus* when John N. Bailey took ownership. The paper still identified as Democratic.

In 1861, the *Peninsular Courier and Ypsilanti Herald* began publication. It carried on as the *Peninsular Courier* less than a year later. In 1866, it continued as the *Peninsula Courier and Family Visitant*. This paper published for ten years before becoming the *Ann Arbor Courier*. In 1899, the paper purchased its main rival, the *Ann Arbor Register* (begun in 1872 by Dr. A.W. Chase) and relaunched as the *Courier-Register*. The Beal family owned and edited the *Courier* for its entire existence, with son Junius taking over for his adoptive father, Rice. The *Courier-Register* continued until 1906. This paper, as well as the Beal family, was staunchly Republican.

The *Ann Arbor Argus-Democrat* formed in 1898 and was a merger of the *Argus*, the *Ann Arbor Democrat* and the *Ypsilanti Weekly Times*. This joint paper ran for eight years before being renamed the *Ann Arbor Weekly Argus*.

FOCUS ON THE BEAL FAMILY

The Beal family had a long history of being politically active. Rice Beal, born in 1823, made his fortune in the lumber business. He went on to publish the *Ann Arbor Courier* and served as the chairman of the Michigan Republican Party. Rice passed away in 1883.

Junius Beal was born to James and Loretta Field in 1860; both parents died before Junius's first birthday. Rice and Phoebe Beal, his uncle and aunt, adopted him and moved the young child to Ann Arbor, where he was educated in the public schools and at the University of Michigan. Junius edited and published the *Courier* after his adoptive father's death, managed

Junius Beal. *Ann Arbor District Library.*

a gas company, directed Ann Arbor's Electric Light Company and served as a presidential elector, a regent for the University of Michigan and a Republican legislator in the Michigan House during the Forty-Third Legislature. After serving in the state legislature, Junius went on to work as the vice president of the Farmers and Mechanics Bank. He passed away in 1942 and is buried in the family plot in Forest Hill Cemetery.

Another newspaper ran as the *Ann Arbor Times* and began publishing in 1903. Five years later, it merged with the *Ann Arbor News-Argus* (which began its life as the *Ann Arbor News* in 1905) and became known as the *Ann Arbor News Times and Argus*. A few months later, it changed names to the *Ann Arbor Times News*, which became the *Ann Arbor Daily News* in January 1928. At the end of 1936, the name was shortened to the one with which most current Ann Arborites are familiar: the *Ann Arbor News*. The paper was published under that name until 2009, eventually ending up in the lovely building at Division and Huron Streets now occupied by the University of Michigan Credit Union.

John Sinclair founded and published a newspaper that eventually became the *Ann Arbor Sun*. Started in 1967 in Detroit, the paper moved to Ann Arbor when the Trans Love Energies commune did. The White Panther Party and the Rainbow People's Party used the paper as their vehicle for disseminating left-wing information. The paper carried information about local news, music and arts until 1976.

In 1986, Laurie Wechter and Ted Sylvester started the *Agenda*, an independent newspaper that served as a forum for left-wing activist groups as well as area nonprofits. Paid subscriptions and advertising subsidized this free monthly periodical.

After the demise of the *Ann Arbor News* as a daily print paper, blogs, print and online publications arose to fill the gap. The *Ann Arbor Chronicle* was a beloved online periodical published by former Old West Side residents Mary Morgan, a former editor of the *Ann Arbor News*, and Dave Askins, her spouse, who edited the *Chronicle*. Its components included a website and a Twitter feed. The *Chronicle* first published on September 2, 2008, and concluded daily reporting until that date in 2014. Dave Askins left Ann

Ann Arbor News Building. *Bentley Historical Library.*

Arbor to continue his print journalism career in South Dakota and then Texas; Mary stayed in Ann Arbor and founded the CivCity Initiative, a nonprofit seeking to increase citizen-government engagement in Ann Arbor and use that experience to drive engagement in other cities. In the early fall of 2018, Morgan announced the winding down of CivCity following the November elections and her intent to live with Askins again in her home state of Indiana.

The *Ann* was a glossy monthly available free of charge at local destinations for seven years in the Ann Arbor area and published by Kyle Poplin, then a Knight-Wallace Fellow (a journalist in residence at the University of Michigan). After six years, the *Ann* attempted to augment the monthly magazine with *ANNthology*, a weekday email aggregation of other local papers and blogs curated by resident Jim McBee. *ANNthology* published for a year until January 2018, when both projects ceased publication.

The *Ann Arbor Metro Times* was a local edition of Detroit's long-running free weekly paper with its own unique articles and event listings. It was available for a couple of years in the 1990s at the *Metro Times*' usual Ann Arbor locations in place of the Detroit edition.

Radio

Several radio stations have called Ann Arbor home. In the 1920s, four radio stations were authorized: WMAX (1922), WQAJ 833 AM (1923), WCBC 1070 AM (1924) and WCBC 1310 AM (1925). Another AM station, WPAG 1050, was authorized in 1946. An FM station, 98.7 WPAG, started in town in 1948. WUOM 91.7 FM in Ann Arbor signed on that same year and continues to this day as Michigan Radio. In March 1962, WOIA 102.9 FM began, eventually becoming today's WWWW country station. On Valentine's Day 1967, WPAG signed on again at the 107.1 FM frequency. In January 1972, WCBN, a freeform student-run radio station, began at 89.5 FM. It moved to 88.3 FM five years later and continues to this day.

The agricultural station for southeast Michigan and northwest Ohio was WPAG 1050 AM, which operated out of the Hutzel Building at the corner of Main and Liberty Streets. Brothers Paul and Art Greene owned the station, and its call letters reflected their names. In the 1960s, the station played Top 40 hits; it transitioned to adult contemporary music in the 1970s. The 1980s brought big band music and, later, country music. In 1987, the station was purchased by Tom Monaghan, who sold it in 1992. Notable personalities

Students working in East Quad radio station in 1952. *Bentley Historical Library.*

included Bob Ufer, who broadcast Michigan football, and popular host Ted Heusel, who spent sixteen years at the station and served as both morning news host and talk show host.

The WJJX AM station studio, started in 1953, operated out of the Michigan Union. Licensed to UM Regents, half of its budget came from the university and the other half from fundraisers. In 1987, a disc jockey made racist comments on a show being broadcast to student residence halls. The university closed the station and added $1 million to its affirmative action budget.

Rock and roll station WIQB 103 FM featured many popular local on-air personalities, including Reid Paxton and Doug Podell, as well as syndicated shows such as *Doctor Demento*. A locally produced show, *Sunday Night Hot Wax*, aired weekly.

WPAG and Bob Ufer. *Bentley Historical Library.*

A sure sign of the influence of the World Wide Web happened in 2002, when AnnArborAlive.com went live. It featured local volunteer DJs and news online but went dormant in 2016. Like WPAG before it, the headquarters were located in the Hutzel Building at Main and Liberty Streets.

Television

The first television station in the county, and the first UHF station in the state, was WPAG-TV, channel 20. It began on April 3, 1953, and was on the air until December 31, 1957. The FCC gave a permit to the University of Michigan in 1953 to air WUOM-TV on channel 26, but it never made it to air. Instead, in 1981, WIHT signed on with some locally produced programming, some syndicated shows and a block of time every day devoted to It Subscription Television, a scrambled TV network with descrambler hardware available for monthly rental. In 1989, the station was sold to Lowell Paxson and became WPXD, an affiliate of the family-friendly Pax TV network, now known as ION Television. Although its transmitter is located in Southfield today (as are most stations serving the Detroit market), its business offices are still in Ann Arbor.

Movies

Since the beginning, Ann Arborites have enjoyed seeing live plays, operas and motion pictures in grand theaters, movie palaces, small theaters and chain cinemas. In 1837—just thirteen years after the Allens and Rumseys settled the town—the Ann Arbor Thespian Society put on shows. Twenty men and women, all amateurs, spent a few months entertaining locals before interest waned and the group disbanded. Interest in live performance apparently sparked four years later, when the Bowery Amphitheater Circus began appearing around town. Despite criticism from the local press and the Presbyterian church, the circus carried on for two years.

Despite the lack of formal theaters, there were still plenty of places to see a show: at Chauncey Goodrich's inn, at a theater opened by two men named Parker and Ellis (apparently only open during the summer, as they were unable to heat it in the winter) and at Hangsterfer Hall.

The real theater scene got started in 1871, when G.D. Hill opened his opera house at Main and Ann Streets. Referred to as both Hill's Opera House and the Athens Opera House, this theater ushered in a new era for our small town. The one-story building hosted musicians, dancers, vaudeville and lectures and boasted that it heated itself with steam and was lit by gas. B.C. Whitney bought the place, added two stories and changed the name to the Whitney Theater, reopening in 1908 with a performance by the Chicago Whitney Opera House Company. To get into the theater, one actually entered through the hotel lobby of the Whitney Hotel, which was next door. One option for getting tickets was to climb the fire escape to reach a ticket window in the second balcony.

Around the time that Whitney was remodeling his theater, dozens of vaudeville and silent movie theaters began to dot the landscape of Ann Arbor. Both the Bijou (209 East Washington Street, which opened in 1906) and the Star (118 East Washington Street, where Arbor Brewing Company is now, opened in 1907) had screens for short films as well as stages for live vaudeville shows.

The Star was the scene of another sort of live show when a riot broke out among students. Several reasons are given: the theater manager kicked out students, an usher made two heckling students leave, boys watching a vaudeville show got too rambunctious, or it was payback for the manager asking a football player to throw a game the prior fall. Whatever the cause might have been, the results were some minor injuries and some major damage to the theater.

Other theaters continued opening during this time. In 1906, the Theatorium opened at 119 East Liberty Street (much later becoming Liberty Street Video rental). Three movies were shown each week for a nickel a show. In December of that year, the Casino opened on Main Street (where

Star Theatre. *Bentley Historical Library.*

the Real Seafood restaurant is now). This theater specifically noted that its offerings would appeal to women and children with shows that "everyone" could enjoy. The next year, the campus-area People's Popular Family Theater began operating at 220 State Street (later a Häagen-Dazs ice cream shop and now a Starbucks).

Eventually, vaudeville faded away as films gained prominence; some theaters in Ann Arbor followed suit, often showing movies for a nickel apiece. However, by the next decade, these so-called nickelodeons continued to be seen as the poor man's show, losing favor with audiences. By the mid-1910s, Ann Arbor saw the Theatorium, Casino and Vaudette become a photography studio, grocery store and shoe repair shop, respectively.

A fancier option for silent films opened in 1907 at 316 Maynard Street. Aptly called the Majestic, this 1,100-seat theater featured a balcony, dressing rooms and confectionery as well as a stage that featured both vaudeville shows and films. Yet another small riot took place—this time because of a vaudeville show that featured a woman sitting in a luminescent moon that appeared to float over the audience. Determined to figure out how this was done, some plucky students brought along flashlights to investigate. The manager instructed his ushers to throw out anyone carrying a flashlight, but before they could do so, the students rushed the manager, pulled him out of the theater to the outside and rolled him in a snowbank. (Two sophomores ended up going to jail; it is not known if the other students ever found out how the trick was done).

As vaudeville faded, the Majestic remained in business and began focusing on movies; the Whitney followed suit. Motion pictures became longer—and better—as the entertainment industry found its new medium. The middle of the decade saw four new theaters open up in downtown Ann Arbor: the Orpheum (1913), the Arcade, the Rae and the Wuerth (1917). Fred Wuerth owned both his namesake theater and the Orpheum (the last remnants of which can be seen as Gratzi's facade) until the 1920s.

One of the complaints about nickelodeons was that they were not appropriate places for children and families. This in part led to the building of movie palaces—extravagant places to watch a motion picture with your family. The first such movie palace in Ann Arbor opened in 1928 and continues to show movies to this day: the legendary Michigan Theater still stands at 603 East Liberty Street. In 1929, the Wuerth debuted its sound system when it showed *The Ghost Talks*. A year later, the Michigan and the Majestic started showing "talkies" as well.

The Majestic Theater. *Bentley Historical Library.*

The Arcade Theater
lit up at night. *Bentley
Historical Library.*

Around this time, both the Arcade and the Rae burned down when the nitrate film ignited. Fred Wuerth continued to operate the Wuerth and Orpheum Theaters, both of which came to be considered pioneers in the era of "one reelers." Things were going well for the theaters until Wuerth leased them to the Butterfield firm in 1923. The firm abandoned the two movie houses in 1957; the Orpheum space eventually became part of Faber's Fabrics, and the Wuerth was later turned into a warehouse before being renovated in the mid-1960s to hold an expansion of Faber's and Fiegel's Men's and Boys' Wear.

The State Theater opened in 1942, premiering with Dorothy Lamour in *The Fleet's In* on a single eighteen-foot-wide screen. It was designed by C. Howard Crane, the architect of Detroit's glamorous Fox Theater. In the fall of 1953, the screen was enlarged to a panorama-ready forty-three feet wide and twenty-four feet high. By the summer of 1979, the management, Butterfield Theaters, had completed a $100,000 project to split the single screen into four separate screening rooms by walling off the middle of each level, enclosing the balcony, and resetting and refurbishing the seats. The theater management believed that with four screens, it could offer more films for longer periods of time. Years before "stadium seating" would become the norm for movie theaters, the upstairs screening rooms were tiered so that no seat was a bad seat—as long as you didn't mind looking a little to the left. In 1984, Butterfield sold the State to George Kerasotes Corporation of Springfield, Illinois. Though Kerasotes would manage the theater for only five more years, its "GKC"-patterned carpeting would remain in the theater for its next acts—as a second-run bargain theater, then managed and programmed by the nearby Michigan Theater as an additional outlet for its arthouse fare as well as cult films and midnight movies. It continues to thrive after a recent remodel.

The Campus Theater opened on South University Avenue in 1957. Perhaps as a sort of reaction to the ornate movie palaces of Main Street, the Campus was sleek and modern. It opened with *Lust for Life*, starring Kirk Douglas, and was popular in the 1960s for foreign film selections. Unlike other area single-screen theaters before and after, it was never divided into multiple screens. It remained as a single thousand-seat auditorium until its 1987 closure to build the South University Galleria. The Campus Theater's neon sign was displayed in the Galleria's food court.

The Fifth Forum (sometimes Romanized as "Vth Forum") was envisioned by its management as an arthouse destination. Its Fifth Avenue location was a magnet for controversy for screening envelope-pushing films like *I Am Curious*

(Yellow). Later it would rebrand as the Ann Arbor 1&2 and book popular films alongside the festival fare. The Ann Arbor 1&2 closed in the summer of 1999 as its parent, Goodrich Quality Theaters, opened the Quality 16 on Jackson Road in Scio Township; the Ann Arbor 1&2's manager joined the management team at the multiplex.

Fox Village Theatre opened in 1967 on the city's west side in the Maple Village shopping center. It was managed by National General, who named it to keep the brand consistent with other famous Fox Theatres it controlled (including Woodward Avenue's Fox Theatre in Detroit and the iconic Fox Westwood Village in Beverly Hills, California). It premiered with one enormous screen; even after its conversion to two screens in 1978, Theater One was still the largest in town for a long time. Two new screening rooms were added in 1979.

By the 1990s, Fox Village was showing some age. Without the selection of a multiplex like Showcase or the stadium seating of the newly opened Quality 16 nearby, it needed a new hook. Its management, United Artists Theatre Circuit, began to program it as a second-run bargain theater. The $1.50 admission ($2.00 on the weekends) goosed attendance, though the concessions remained at first-run prices. The theater continued as a second-run venue under various management until the spring of 2005, when the Village Theatre (the final owners dropped the Fox name) finally closed for good. The theaters were gutted and the space reopened in 2007 as Plum Market, an upscale grocery from the family that formerly operated Merchant of Vino on Plymouth Road.

In 1974, a Michigan student film organization was chafing at new event restrictions enacted by university administration and searched for a venue near campus to continue film screening. It landed a lease on the former Mark's Coffeehouse at 605 East William Street and opened in the winter of 1975 as the Matrix Theater. The group initially programmed popular films to build up savings but eventually pivoted to the arthouse and foreign fare formerly screened in campus auditoriums. Legend tells that the management was lax on enforcing rating restrictions for younger patrons.

University Drive-In was located at 4100 Carpenter Road and was managed by Butterfield. Reportedly, it cost $500,000 to build and boasted a car capacity of 1,033. The drive-in opened in July 1965, was sold to National Amusements in 1984 and shut down for good in 1987. Showcase Cinemas soon opened on the site with fourteen screens.

The Scio Drive-In, located at 6588 Jackson Road, opened in 1953 with a seven-hundred-car capacity. The drive-in showed adult films in 1974–75, closed for good in 1986 and was demolished five years later. It is currently vacant land for sale, and the old driveway to the theater can be seen on Google Street View.

The Movies at Briarwood opened in 1973 along with its titular mall, following a pattern of United Artists theaters inside Detroit-area malls managed by the Taubman Companies (others included the Movies at Fairlane, in Dearborn; the Movies at Prudential Town Center, in Southfield; and the Movies at Twelve Oaks, in Novi.) United Artists decided to follow the industry trend toward larger theaters and began to leave Detroit-area malls in the early 2000s when it was acquired by a larger chain, Regal Entertainment Group. As of 2018, the only United Artists theater in southeast Michigan is the UA Commerce Stadium 14, a freestanding multiplex and Costco neighbor near M-5 in Commerce Township.

After United Artists pulled out of Ann Arbor, its space was given a quick coat of paint and reopened in September 2002, now managed by Madstone, an up-and-coming chain that touted itself as "a different kind of cinematic experience for a different kind of moviegoer. Instead of the mainstream popcorn flicks that used to be in the space, Madstone's theater will be… [an] exhibition of independent, art-adjacent, specialty and foreign films." The theater closed in June 2004. Some of the films shown during its brief run were *Dr. Strangelove*, *The Cabinet of Dr. Caligari* and *Citizen Kane*, alongside selected "quality" popular films like the *Lord of the Rings* trilogy.

The last phase of the Briarwood theaters was as a four-screen dollar theater managed by Teicher Theatres, a second-run chain with other locations in Ohio, Indiana and Florida. (Three of the screening rooms were converted to storage and break rooms for mall tenants.) Briarwood ended Teicher's lease when MC Sports, a Michigan sporting goods chain, expressed interest in moving to the mall; MC removed the walls and converted the theaters' footprint into a single open space for its wares. The entire MC Sports chain collapsed in 2016; its former Briarwood space is now occupied by seasonal pop-up merchants and attractions.

The industry's shift to digital projection currently makes dollar theaters infeasible; Alan Teicher, who operated Briarwood before its closure, cited an upgrade cost of $50,000 per screen before he closed his remaining theaters. There is currently only one dollar theatre in southeastern Michigan.

4

FIND WHAT YOU NEED

From Dry Goods Stores to Locally Owned Shops to Chain Stores

BOOKSTORES FROM WAHR'S TO BORDERS TO CHAINS

Ann Arbor loves its books. Even today, with bookstores closing and e-books increasing in popularity, Ann Arbor boasts numerous bookstores—and it turns out that we've been book lovers from the start.

As early as 1844, a bookstore operated in Lower Town across from a flouring mill. William R. Perry, an avid abolitionist and pal of the publisher of *Signal of Liberty*, was the owner and operator. An advertisement in 1855 announced that Wilmot & Company had bought the stock of A.B. Wood and would sell it "at the old stand" on North Main Street opposite the courthouse, just north of the Franklin Block.

Both the *Michigan Argus* and the *Ann Arbor Argus* mention, without much detail, several other booksellers around in the early days: Moore, Sheehan & Andrews; Sheehan's and Wahr's; Douglass & Company (1879); and Moore and Osius (1885). In 1891, Moore and Taber's Book Stores advertised their locations at 6 South Main Street and at William and State Street. Just a year before, Moore and Wetmore advertised their bookstores at these same locations, saying they sold books as well as "lawn tennis and base ball goods [and] hammocks"; it is unclear what happened to Mr. Wetmore.

While not much is known about some stores or their owners, we do know quite a bit about George Wahr. Wahr opened a bookstore in either 1888 or 1890, depending on the source. Unlike the opening date, the location is not

The Wahr's bookstore sign is visible in this Main Street picture. *Bentley Historical Library.*

in dispute: it was on Main Street across from the courthouse and in the same block as the opera house. A second location opened on State Street in 1894.

The son of German pioneers who arrived in 1835, Wahr began working in a bookstore in 1875 at the age of fourteen. With two partners, he purchased the store in 1882, and he bought out the partners five years later. His specialty was student supplies, stationery and books. In addition, Wahr operated a successful publishing business that published such items as a map of Ann Arbor and its wards, University of Michigan calendars and poetry tracts.

Wahr's lucrative endeavors enabled him to build a series of homes, some of which still stand today. At South Fourth Avenue near Packard Street, Wahr built a Victorian home featuring elaborate displays of bays, gables, dormers and sunbursts. Just four years later, Wahr moved to what was then the other side of town. The rumored reason for the move was that a neighbor angered Wahr when the neighbor hung his wash outside to dry. While it is possible that Wahr was upset enough to pick up stakes and move, it is also likely that his increasing wealth led to the decision as well. Wahr purchased a property at 126 North Division Street at a tax auction in 1892. After he

Wahr's bookstore in 1970. *Bentley Historical Library.*

and his wife, Emma Staebler Wahr, moved in, they found the inside to their disliking. They quickly cleared a space to the south of the new house and began building a Queen Anne–style home on the side lot. The couple moved in and leased the house at 126 to sororities and fraternities.

Wahr passed away in 1945. His store on State Street continued in some form or another until the Borders brothers bought it in 1972.

Borders Books, of course, was one of Ann Arbor's signature businesses. Started in 1971, the first location was on the second floor of 211 South State Street. This was the first such venture for the Borders brothers, who obtained a $5,000 loan from a friend to get themselves set up. Things began to move quickly—both literally and figuratively. In August 1972, the brothers moved to 316 South State Street (the former location of Wahr's, now the Red Hawk). Two years later, they moved to the former Wagner clothing store at 303 South State Street (most recently the M Den). In 1994, the bookstore moved to the former Jacobson's building (now home to Sweetwaters, Knight's and Hopcat).

The ground floor was filled with books, periodicals and some gift items. The second floor contained two discrete music sections, one for popular music and one for classical titles; a movie section; stationery, more gifts and some nonfiction specialty books; and a café. Displays and shelves could be moved quickly to set up performance spaces for visiting musicians. A band or singer with an evening concert at the Michigan Theater would often perform a quick acoustic set and sign items at Borders earlier in the day. These performances were often recorded and broadcast to other Borders stores and showcased as part of Borders' online series, *Live at 01.* (The downtown store was known internally as "01" as the flagship store in the Borders chain and a symbolic representation of Borders' beginnings nearby.)

In December 2002, the workers at Borders' flagship store voted for union representation. After months of negotiations, the workers went on strike in November of the following year. Thanks to much support from United Food and Commercial Workers Local 876, other local unions and the Ann Arbor community, the matter settled in December 2003. Author Patti Smith recalls bringing homemade treats to the supporters and being encouraged to see that she was not the only person to do so.

The unionization was just one of the many changes over the years. Kmart Corporation acquired Borders for $125 million in 1992 as part of an effort to diversify into specialty stores (other sister chains included OfficeMax and the Sports Authority). Three years later, the corporate headquarters moved to Tally Hall, and later, they moved to Phoenix Drive. In 2011, Borders filed for Chapter 11 bankruptcy protection. In September of that year, the flagship store in Ann Arbor closed.

An entire book could be written about the many bookstores that have graced our city. Until then, here are some that made lasting impressions.

University Cellar was a student-run bookstore in the basement of the Michigan Union and later on Liberty Street. In 1969, students occupied an administration building, demanding a student-run bookstore. The Michigan State Police were called in and arrested some of the student protesters. The University of Michigan Board of Regents approved the creation and capitalized the endeavor partly with money from the Student Vehicle Fund. To shield the regents from any liability arising from the store, a separate corporation was established. University Cellar Inc. remained in the basement of the student union until 1982. During that time, its workers voted to be represented by the International Workers of the World (IWW) Local 660. At the time, it was the largest local, comprising about 10 percent of the union's worldwide membership. After moving to East Liberty Street, the bookstore continued for almost five years, closing in December 1986. The following February, the parent company of Ulrich's took over and reopened the store as Michigan Book and Supply.

Shaman Drum opened in 1980 and specialized in humanities textbooks as well as other general fiction and nonfiction books. This beloved bookstore closed in 2009.

Kaleidoscope Books and Collectibles opened in 1990, specializing in "all the things your mother made you throw away." Its original storefront was on State Street just north of the State Theater. The close proximity to the Power Center, the Michigan Theater and Hill Auditorium compelled visiting entertainers, including Sir Patrick Stewart and Bob Dylan, to stop in and browse. In 2008, proprietor Jeff Pickell moved to 200 North Fourth Avenue, formerly home of the Wooden Spoon, another used bookstore with a focus on cookbooks. Pickell often sat outside this location with tables of marked-down items to encourage foot traffic to venture into the store. Kaleidoscope maintained a presence on Fourth

Left: Shaman Drum. *Bentley Historical Library.*

Below: David's Books. *Bentley Historical Library.*

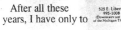
Dawn Treader advertisement. *Ann Arbor District Library.*

Avenue until early 2017, when Pickell retired from retail, though he still sells some rare items online.

While the Dawn Treader shop still exists, it is not in its original location. The bookstore began life on South University Avenue in a space that later became the Underworld Comics & Collectibles (which was owned and managed by science fiction writer Nisi Shawl). A second location opened at Liberty Street near Maynard Street in a space that was below street level. The space is remembered by coauthor Britain Woodman as a "ridiculous labyrinth of shelves, but lots of fun to browse." It later became the Digital Ops gaming facility and then the All Hands Active makerspace. At that time, the store had a wall with envelopes from customers and vendors with myriad misspellings of the store's name ("Dawn Tjader," "Down Treader," and more).

Located at State and Liberty Streets, David's Books commissioned the famous mural on Liberty Street in 1984. The store later moved to William Street between Maynard and Thompson Streets. In addition to selling textbooks and general trade books, there was also a big, roped-off corner of the store that sold "blue" magazines.

RED-LIGHT DISTRICT

Walking on Fourth Avenue today, visitors are treated to the sight of restaurants, a sporting goods store, a cell phone store and other retail establishments. Years ago, a visitor would have seen bookstores of a different kind—the kind that led to Fourth Avenue to be called "two blocks of vice" by local law enforcement. In 1970, the Ann Arbor Adult News and the

This page and opposite: These pictures show various businesses in what had come to be known as the red-light district in the 1970s and 1980s. *Bentley Historical Library.*

Fourth Avenue Adult News opened up right next to each other, at 215 and 217 respectively. Located above both bookstores was the American Massage Parlor, and around the corner at 212 West Huron Street was another parlor called Caesar's Retreat.

The operation of these businesses attracted an unsavory clientele, and both neighbors and the City of Ann Arbor were eager to put a stop to the traffic. Police conducted raids and made arrests, but those did little to slow the illegal activities. Thus, in 1978, the city council passed an ordinance: "Regulations concerning adult entertainment businesses." This new law required the bookstores and massage parlors to obtain licenses and eject any minors on the premises. Even with this new ordinance, the Danish News, complete with a twenty-five-cent movie arcade, began operating at 209 North Fourth Avenue in 1980.

In the early 1980s, the city used zoning ordinances and escalating rents to try to force the businesses out. Raids and lawsuits began to wear down the bookstore and massage parlor owners—and deplete their bank accounts— but the stress was still not enough to make their businesses unprofitable.

In 1986, deep-pocketed local businessmen formed the 200 Fourth Avenue Group to put an end to the red-light district by buying up properties and raising lease rates on adult bookstores and services to drive them out; they would then rejuvenate the area with more appropriate businesses. The last adult business was evicted in 1988 to make way for Fourth Avenue

Birkenstock, bringing Ann Arbor's red-light district to a close after nearly two decades.

Other than having a colorful name, the Blue Front was not associated with the red-light district—at least not officially. Described as the quintessential 1950s corner store, the Blue Front sold liquor, beer, wine and snacks in its later years and penny candy, comic books, paperbacks and children's toys in its early days. It also sold adult magazines and books as well as newspapers from all over the world (for a long time it was the only local place to get a *New York Times*).

Shoppers recall it as a fun place to shop, often in disarray and with an owner who gave you a look if you browsed a little bit too long. Located on a corner at 701 Packard Street, the Blue Front closed its doors in 2014. An upscale craft beer and wine store is now in the location and bears the same name.

OTHERS

Many other independent bookstores operated in Ann Arbor, such as the Book Stop and Community Newscenter (one location in Liberty Plaza and one at South University and Forest Avenues). Keith Orr, former co-owner of \aut\ BAR, says, "Before there was a *Between the Lines Newspaper* or *Out Post*, (and before the internet), news of the gay world came from the *Bay Area Reporter*, the *Washington Blade*, the *Gay Community News*, the *Advocate* (when it wasn't a glossy), and others. The only place to get these in Ann Arbor was the Community News. Can't tell you how important it was to a large number of people."

There was also Bob Marshall's, Follett's, Slater's (which closed in 1972 after fifty-six years in operation; it was located where Bivouac is now), Laco Bookstores Inc., Circle Books (an occult bookstore located at 215 South State Street), Paideia (State Street), State Street Book Shop, Webster's Books (Newscenter's attempt at an upscale bookstore, located on Plymouth Road), Logos Books, Women's Bookstore (225 East Liberty Street), the Wooden Spoon, the Book Stop (2775 Plymouth Road), Charing Cross Books, Centicore Book Shop (336 Maynard Street), Eye of Agamotto Comic Book Shop, Meridian Books (215 South State Street; it specialized in occult and metaphysical tomes), After Words (specializing in closeout and overstock books, with recent and classic books for huge discounts; the space is now

Community Newscenter. *Bentley Historical Library.*

Logos Books on South University Avenue. *Bentley Historical Library.*

occupied by the Vault of Midnight), the Overbeck Book Store (which opened in 1945 at 1216 South University Avenue; the owner worked at Wahr's and then opened his own shop), Dave's II Comics & Collectibles (an extension of popular Royal Oak store at corner of State and William Streets, above what is now Jimmy John's), Michigan Book & Supply (in the former Kresge location at State Street and North University Avenue and closed in 2010s for a new Walgreens) and Zondervan Family Bookstore (a Christian bookstore).

Chains included Waldenbooks, B. Dalton and its successor Doubleday Book Company at Briarwood, Little Professor (now Nicola's) and the Children's Bookmark (a Detroit-area chain).

Dr. Chase, Publisher

Many bestselling writers have called Ann Arbor home, but one of the most engaging was Dr. Alvin Wood Chase. Originally from a farm in New York State, Chase left home as a teenager to peddle household drugs and groceries in an area that would later become known as Toledo, Ohio. During his travels, Chase picked up handwritten recipes and medical remedies that he copied and sold to his customers. He settled in Ann Arbor in 1856, still selling his recipes. Chase had no formal medical training when he began attending medical lectures at the university; however, two years later, he received a degree from the Eclectic Medical Institute in Cincinnati after just sixteen weeks of study. (The new doctor is said to have finished at the head of his class.)

Within just two years after receiving this degree, Dr. Chase was a widely respected and esteemed physician. In 1863, he published *Dr. A.W. Chase's Recipes*. The book shared recipes for everything from "oatmeal-aid" to soap to vinegar to medicines to hair restoration. He also included a cure for cholera, relief for asthma, directions on how to make a sheepskin mat, a way to get your cow to produce more milk and how to make fly "stickumfast." While Chase did not write most of these recipes, he did compile and edit them and became one of the city's richest men.

Dr. Chase also wrote books that were considered some of the most popular tomes of the nineteenth century, publishing dozens of editions in both English and German. All the while, Dr. Chase continued to travel, practice medicine, sell his book and deliver an estimated three thousand babies.

Left: Dr. Alvin Chase. *Bentley Historical Library.*

Below: Dr. Chase's Steam Printing House, at Main and Miller Streets, was later a Montgomery Ward warehouse. *Bentley Historical Library.*

Using the money he earned, Dr. Chase opened Dr. Alvin Wood Chase's Steam Printing House at the corner of Miller and Main Streets. According to Dr. Chase himself, this was the "finest printing office in the West," with a press room, counting room, job room and bindery. Each of these rooms was thirty-nine feet by sixty-eight feet "in the clear, without a partition in any of them." To protect this beautiful investment, Dr. Chase took great pains to prevent against fire. These measures included placing one hundred feet of firehose near the steam pump as well as an additional twenty-five feet of firehose in each of the other rooms.

In 1869, Chase sold all of his Ann Arbor holdings to newspaper editor Rice Beal and retired to Minnesota. But you can't keep a good doctor down, and within a few years, Chase created a new book, including advice on how to keep bees. He returned to Ann Arbor to publish it but was quickly stopped by Beal, who got an injunction for breach of contract. Chase and his financial backers simply set up business in Toledo and, to get around the contractual issues, bought out the doctor's share. Unfortunately, Chase did not share in the profits and died during his attempt to find a publisher for the third version of his book, which ultimately was published posthumously by F.B. Dickerson of Detroit in 1898.

Incredibly, over four million copies of his book were ultimately printed and sold; the book continues its life as part of the Google Books project.

Dry Goods Stores and Grocery Stores

In the early days of Ann Arbor, residents shopped in dry goods stores. They dotted the landscape of our downtown: Miller and Pray (300 North Main Street), Rinsey-Seabolt (114–116 West Washington Street), Blaich & Gates, Blaich Brothers, Overbeck & Staebler, Rinsey & Seabolt's (113 East Washington Street), Rinsey's Grocery (South Fourth Avenue and East Huron Street), Farmers' Sheds Grocery (at Catherine and Main Streets), Charles Pardon's butcher shop and grocery store (219–223 North Main Street, built between 1894 and 1899), Calkins Fletcher (Packard and State Streets) Fischer & Finnell (also at Packard and State Streets), Staebler & Company, Excelsior Grocery (11 East Ann Street), Herrick and Bohnet (208 North Fourth Avenue), Bach & Abel, B. St. James, Goodyear & St. James, Jack's Market (1028 East University Avenue), Grennan & Clague (Packard Street and Dewey Avenue) and perhaps the best known of the bunch, Dean & Company.

Bach & Abel. *Bentley Historical Library.*

Fischer & Finnell grocery and cigar shop sat on a corner of Packard Road and State Street. James Finnell was also an auctioneer. *Bentley Historical Library.*

Dean & Company. *Bentley Historical Library.*

Located at 214 South Main Street, Dean & Company started during the Civil War and continued as a wholesaler until after World War I. While the store began as a seller of dry goods, it soon focused on the finer things in life, specializing in luxuries of the day such as fine chinaware. Sedgwick Dean embarked on regular trips to New York to find the best coffee, which he then brought home and roasted in the basement of the store. He also sold pipe and chewing tobacco but eschewed cigarettes. Other perishables included crackers, oranges and lemons, bananas, bulk raisins and prunes, oatmeal, flour, sugar, vinegar and molasses. Customers spoke of fancy cheeses displayed beneath glass and of hot roasted peanuts available for a nickel. When it became evident that the car would be king, Dean installed a gas pump in front of his store and had clerks bring out cans of gasoline to fill up the tanks of passing motorists.

For decades, the Hertler siblings—Gotleib, Emma, Herman and George—provided gardening and farming advice to interested customers, a place to leave your horse (for just a dime) and euchre games for friends and customers. The building still stands and is the home of the very popular

FOCUS ON ELIZABETH DEAN

Elizabeth Dean. *Bentley Historical Library.*

Before her death in 1964, Elizabeth Russell Dean was a quiet citizen in our fair city. The daughter of one of the owners of the Dean & Company general store, Elizabeth spent her entire life in Ann Arbor. Apparently, she didn't put on airs and didn't attend all of the happening gatherings—but what she did do changed the look of our city in ways most of us can't even fathom, let alone achieve.

Elizabeth's mother died when she was born (it is not clear if she died in childbirth or shortly thereafter), so the young girl was raised by a maternal aunt called Mrs. Stebbins and nursemaids. She and sister Clara, who was nine years her senior, grew up at 120 Packard Street. The homestead was a large home built around 1860 by early settler Wallace Wines, who later sold it to his son-in-law Sedgwick.

The home was close to Main Street and thus not far from the family store. Sedgwick would often take his carriage home to find his younger daughter on the front steps waiting for a handful of those famous hot peanuts. A fiercely independent young woman, Elizabeth reportedly did not like school and quit high school before graduating. She enjoyed traveling but was always extremely loyal to her hometown of Ann Arbor.

After World War I, Elizabeth sold her family home to a local Lutheran minister. At some point, she lived in the Anberay apartments at 619 East University Avenue. Eventually, she lived in a home at 1021 Vaughan Street. Elizabeth R. Dean passed away at her home in 1964, when she was seventy-nine years old; she never married and had no children. From the few articles about her, it sounds like she had a good life—perhaps even a wonderful one.

If not for what happened next, people would likely have still remembered Elizabeth fondly, but eventually her memory would have faded along with the memories of that fancy store on Main Street. However, Elizabeth did something that most of us are not be able to, and she did it not for herself but for the betterment of her beloved hometown.

Dean's will left nearly $2 million to the City of Ann Arbor to be held in a separate fund, the income used for the care, maintenance and replacement of trees on city-owned property. News reports indicate that our city council was "stunned" upon the reading of her will and learning of this extreme generosity. Almost immediately, some questioned her exact intent—did she want her gift to provide for special projects and tree care beyond what was provided in the regular budget, or should it be included in the forestry department's regular budget? The city councilmembers in the 1960s interpreted her will to provide for special care beyond the normal budget of the forest department and carried out this request with several major tree-planting projects.

In 1965, a three-block promenade was installed on the 200 block of South Main Street. Four dozen planter boxes contained moraine honey locusts and leaf lindens, and four other planter boxes contained shrubs. Brick walkways lined the street between the planter boxes, along with drinking fountains and benches. In following years, the city used the income to match federal beautification grants and to help with insect control. A plaque honors her gift to our city.

City council established the Dean Fund Committee in 1975. The members of the committee make recommendations to the council on how to spend the interest generated by the trust fund. Proposals for ideas come from neighborhood associations, merchants and citizens—anyone can submit a request. The fund has been responsible for planting over 5,400 trees along city streets and in city parks and has helped to repair, maintain and otherwise care for thousands of trees across the city.

Downtown Home & Garden store. When former owner Mark Hodesh purchased the business in 1975, Emma Hertler was still running it; her brothers Herman and Gotleib were in the Huron View Nursing Home. Among other gems, the building contains the last horse stalls in downtown Ann Arbor. When asked if there are many pictures of the Hertler family,

Hertler Brothers at 210 South Ashley Street. *Ann Arbor District Library.*

Hodesh said that there aren't many around because they didn't like having their pictures taken—they would have rather been working!

As dry goods stores faded away, grocery stores filled the need for food and supplies. The thriving climate and growing city of Ann Arbor was home to some longtime grocers. For thirty-seven years, seven days a week, twelve hours a day, Thomas Kussurelis worked at the grocery store bearing his name. Located at 619 North Main Street, the store was opened during the Great Depression and weathered on until 1963, when Kussurelis sold the shop and retired.

When Daniel Haas opened his grocery store at 114 West Liberty Street in 1904, he likely did not realize he would one day be the oldest grocer in the city, but that is exactly what happened. Haas began his career working at Rinsey & Seabolt's as a clerk, briefly worked in the insurance business and launched the Haas & Heibein store at 207 South Main Street just four years after the turn of the century. After the dissolution of the partnership in 1918, Haas moved to the Liberty Street location and carried on business until 1949. He passed away in 1957 at the age of eighty-two.

Miner Street Grocery at 614 Miner Street. *Ann Arbor District Library.*

The Campus Smoke Shop, at the corner of Maynard and East Liberty Streets, remained in the Eskin family for two decades until its demise in 1969. Generations of locals bought their *New York Times* and *Ann Arbor News* there, along with tobacco and actual corncob pipes. Jacob Eskin passed away at ninety-one in 1988.

Corner grocery stores were many in Ann Arbor. This list is not exhaustive but hopefully will evoke memories of trips to the store to get milk for dinner, wax lips, baseball cards or just a cold drink on a hot summer's day: Van's Market (602 South Main Street); K&S Market (609 West Jefferson Street across from Bach Elementary; if you got a red-and-yellow gumball, you won a candy bar); McCoy's Market (Thomas Kussurelis sold them his store on North Main Street); Yarmain's (Dexter and Jackson Avenues); Fox's (Miller Avenue and Brooks Street); Murphy's (Dexter Avenue); Strickland's (1352 Geddes Avenue); Grennan & Clague, which eventually became Clague's Grocery (1200 Packard Street, now Argus Farm Stop); Schlegel Grocery, later Ted's Grocery (524 South Second Street); Dean's Market (Second Street); Nick's (Chapin Street and Miller Avenue); Greg's (Spring and

Hiscock Streets); Brooks Market (Brooks Street and Miller Avenue); Jefferson Market (Jefferson Street, near Bach School); Summit Street Grocery (Main and Summit Streets); Main Street Grocery (Miller Avenue and Ann Street); Dieroff's Market (Detroit Street, where Zingerman's Deli is now); Tom's Grocery (Felch and North Main Streets); Leverette's Market (Platt Road and Packard Street); Johnny's (Jefferson Street); Corner Grocery (Miller Avenue and Chapin Street); Food & Drug (Packard Street and Stadium Boulevard); Freeman's Grocery; Capitol Market (211 South Fourth Avenue); Buster's (3050 Platt Road); Fraternity Market (1308 South University Avenue); Bill's Korner Market (820 Miller Avenue); Consumer's Beef and Cheese; Vescio's, National and Wrigley's (all at Liberty Street and Stadium Boulevard); Food Mart (Church Street and South University Avenue); Miner Street Grocery; Coleman's Market (Washtenaw Avenue and Pittsfield Boulevard); Fireside Food Company (The Yellow Barn at 410 West Huron Street); Stephen's (East University and South University Avenues); McDougall's Grocery (1123 South University Avenue); Milk Depot (Maple Road and Dexter Avenue); and White Market (William Street, near the Diag; now Hunter House Hamburgers).

The Great Atlantic & Pacific Tea Company, also known as A&P, had a store at 115–117 West Washington Street. *Bentley Historical Library.*

Consumer's Beef and Cheese, at 216 West Huron Street, carried wholesale and retail cheese, beef and seafood. *Ann Arbor District Library.*

Chain stores could also be found around town. A Kroger grocery store was located at Main and Ann Streets, where the old post office had been. A&P could be found at several locations around town, including on East Stadium Boulevard and South Industrial Highway and downtown at 115–117 West Washington Street (where Logan and Frita Batidos are today). While Kroger continues to this day, the Great Atlantic and Pacific Tea Company is long gone. The chain of stores that became known as A&P began as a mail-order tea business in 1859, and by the turn of the century, there were twenty stores in the A&P chain. In its heyday, the company had thousands of markets all over the country. There was also a short-lived Piggly-Wiggly on Packard Street that eventually became the Packard Pharmacy (then a bicycle store and now part of the Zen Buddhist temple). The Michigan-based chain of Hiller's grocery stores also had a location in Ann Arbor at Arborland.

DRUGSTORES

Druggists and pharmacies dotted the landscape of early Ann Arbor, some carrying things that would now (and maybe even then) be considered dubious. Eberbach & Sons (at 112 South Main Street) carried the Elixir of Youth, which its producers guaranteed was a "positive cure" for "Loss of Power" afflicting men of a certain age.

Bach & Abel sold Burdock Blood Bitters, which the discoverer claimed did not cure *all* ills; nevertheless, it cured every illness arising from "a torpid liver, impure blood, disordered kidneys." A.E. Mummery brought customers Zoa Phora, which claimed that what it couldn't cure for womankind, "no medicine will." Goodyear & Company shelved an item called Catarrh Remedy that claimed to cure deafness just ten minutes after application.

Calkins Pharmacy, with locations on South University Avenue and State Street, carried a dyspepsia cure that guaranteed to cure what ailed folks. Palmer's Pharmacy on South State Street was the place to go for all of your Pabst Blue Ribbon extract needs, as seen in the picture on the following page from 1896.

Of course, these pharmacies carried legitimate items as well and often featured that staple of old-fashioned goodness: the soda counter. Brown's

Mummery's Drug Store, on the corner of East Washington Street and South Fourth Avenue, around 1910; the building was known as the "Washington Block." *Bentley Historical Library.*

Pabst Blue Ribbon extract for sale in 1896 at Palmer's Pharmacy on South State Street. *Bentley Historical Library.*

Pharmacy, at Packard and Wells Streets, asserted that it was the "only" one serving up whipped cream and soda in 1890. Hale and Tremain's drugstore and soda shop diversified a bit by opening up an insurance agency on the premises. Mann's Drug Store, at 213 South Main Street, advertised in 1899 that it had some amazing vanilla beans that were "absolutely pure of their own making" and warned against getting vanilla made from chemicals.

In 1930, Frederick Stegath opened Stegath's Drug Store on South University Avenue. Oscar Carlson bought the pharmacy after Stegath's death and renamed it after himself. Decades later, Fred Kreye bought the store and called it the Village Apothecary. That name, harkening back to ancient medicine men and women, stuck until the pharmacy closed in April 2015.

Also on South University Avenue were Witham's and Wikel; these two stores were located kitty-corner from each other at Forest Avenue. Witham's Drugs was built around 1929. In 1970, Witham's was replaced by Village Corner, known for its wine selection and counterculture atmosphere. Village Corner thrived in the location until construction forced a move to the north side of town. Decades before any of this happened, John Dewey,

At first, Christian Eberbach worked in the W.S. Maynard store, but in 1842, he founded Eberbach and Company to manufacture articles sold by pharmacists and opened the Eberbach Drug Store on Main Street. *Bentley Historical Library.*

the philosopher and educator, moved into a brick Italianate home at this location. He began his residence in 1889 and left five years later.

Swift Drugs, at 340 South State Street (now State Street Liquors), became Wikel-Schurz Drugs in 1957. Byron W. Swift operated the drugstore beginning in 1925 after starting in the pharmacy business in 1921 as a partner of L.O. Cushing. Swift died in 1956, and Howard L. Wikel and Daniel H. Schurz bought the business from his estate.

Other pharmacies included Bassett Brothers on State Street; Cushing's, which prided itself on selling copious amounts of candy; and A.C. Schumacher, who advertised his vast selection of perfumes.

Located in the Maple Village on the west side of town, the Village Pharmacy II opened in 1998 and closed in 2015. The business was sold to Walgreens, but a physical store never materialized; instead, Walgreens just acquired the prescription records of former customers.

The Quarry, founded by James Quarry, began as a small drugstore in 1898. Its original location was on North University Avenue and State Street,

Quarry Drug around 1929, located at North University Avenue and State Street. *Bentley Historical Library.*

the spot eventually occupied by Kresge. By 1972, the Quarry boasted three locations: 320 South State Street, 2355 East Stadium Boulevard and 2215 West Stadium Boulevard. In that year, the small chain was sold to Ypsilanti druggist Joseph Decker, who owned two Richardson Pharmacies; he later renamed the drugstore to Richardson. The Quarry name lived on, however, with its hospital supply store that opened in 1939 and camera supply store that opened in 1951.

On South University Avenue, pharmacist Robert Lumbard operated Lumbard's University Drug Store from 1952 to 1962. Lumbard passed away in 1968.

The corner of Main and Madison Streets housed several drugstores, starting with Kolander's, then Pritchard's, then Yates and later Michigan Drug. Long after the drugstores had left, the building burned to the ground in 2014.

The Prescription Shop, located in the Ann Arbor Professional Building at 423 East Washington Street (now the Varsity apartment tower), had the distinction of being the last independent pharmacy downtown, closing in 2008.

Owner Tom Kundrat bought Wenk's Pharmacy from Fred Wenk and consolidated the two stores and their respective clientele into Wenk's building on East Stadium Boulevard, calling the new business Wenk's Prescription Shop. The business is now part of the Hometown Pharmacy chain.

Mindells Pharmacy, on the southwest corner of Packard Street and Carpenter Road, opened in 1967 and closed in 1995, when Arbor Drugs bought it. After closing Mindells, the Arbor Drugs company opened a franchise just north of where Mindells had been.

James A. O'Sullivan opened the first Cunningham's Drugstore in Detroit. He opened a Food and Drug Mart in Ypsilanti in 1947 and then came to Ann Arbor with a location at Packard Street and Stadium Boulevard in 1950. He opened a Food Mart at 1123 South University Avenue, replacing McDougall's Grocery, which closed after sixty years in business. In 1965, O'Sullivan bought Fenn's Drug Store at 103 Forest Avenue. (Clare Fenn was at the time of the sale the city's oldest owner-druggist and also a former city alderman.) The Food and Drug Mart on Stadium Boulevard featured a lunch counter, a frozen food section, dairy, produce and dry goods. It also filled prescriptions until 1998, when Jim O'Sullivan (son of James) sold his inventory to Arbor Drugs. The market carried on a while longer; the site of the much-missed Food and Drug Mart now hosts several businesses including a convenience store.

Other drugstores in the area included Lucky Drugs (Main Street near Liberty Street; it later became Joy Pharmacy), Collins Pills'n'Things, Cunningham Drugs (at Liberty and Main Streets in the space of Mack & Company and where Pretzel Bell is now) and chains such as Perry Drugs (later Rite Aid Pharmacy) and Arbor Drugs (later CVS), which had locations all over town.

Co-Ops

For a time, North Fourth Avenue was a bastion of food co-ops: People's Produce, Wildflour Bakery (a worker collective and thus technically not a cooperative in the sense the others were), the Tofu Factory and the People's Food Co-Op (PFC) all occupied the block. These uniquely structured entities allowed shoppers to also be owners of the business. The first to open was in 1971, when the People's Food Co-Op began selling goods on an honor system. It started with a folding table on State Street, moved to

People's Food Co-Op on Packard Street on its closing night. *Author's collection.*

a basement space and finally relocated to a house at 722 Packard Street. Throughout the years, the venerable PFC has gone from an all-volunteer staff to paid employees, a formalized membership structure and an expanded space that includes a coffeehouse. It remains in business to this day at 216 North Fourth Avenue.

In November 1976, the People's Produce Co-Op opened at 206 North Fourth Avenue (where Tea Haus is currently located). Much like the original food co-op, this new co-op had no paid staff and relied on volunteer day coordinators. Around the same time, the Ann Arbor Tofu Collective (later called the Soy Plant) started to produce tofu for sale in the co-ops. In 1978, the Daily Grind opened at 220 Felch Street (where the Ann Arbor Distillery is now). In 1978, the People's Herb and Spice Co-Op opened at 211 Ann Street (now Eat More Tea).

The Wildflour Community Bakery remains in the fond memories of legions of Ann Arborites. Many community volunteers joined the paid staff in creating pizza dough, bread, cookies and muffins. It also did not have a formal membership, and anyone could attend the community meetings and vote on all of the issues. One hour of work entitled one to a 17 percent discount on twenty dollars' worth of food; working an hour and a half earned

Left: Applerose Natural Food, around 1971, located at 404 West Liberty Street. *Ann Arbor District Library.*

Right: Another option for organic food in the 1970s was ShakLee. Note the sign for a waterbed store. *Bentley Historical Library.*

a free loaf of bread in addition to the discount. At one point, a volunteer could earn a loaf of bread for working a two-hour shift. The beloved bakery closed in 1997 but is credited as an inspiration for Avalon Bakery.

Other options for natural and organic foods included Applerose Natural Foods at 404 West Liberty Street, ShakLee and a market that shared space with the Seva vegetarian restaurant.

DEPARTMENT STORES

There have been many department stores in Ann Arbor, beginning with Mack & Company and continuing through the decades to include such beloved stores as Goodyear's, Kline's, Fiegel's, Hutzel's and Muehlig's—all gone but hopefully not forgotten.

Located at the northwest corner of Main and Liberty Streets and founded in 1860, Mack & Company was the largest department store in the city at one time. Founder Christian Mack came to Ann Arbor in 1851 and worked for a local merchant, opening his own store in 1857. The store, initially known as Mack & Schmid, began by selling dry goods, groceries and yard implements, eventually growing into household goods and dry goods only. The store originally had a bargain basement and, at the beginning of its existence, was one of only two department stores in the state that could sell prescription drugs. The store, which started at 3,700 square feet, eventually grew to over 100,000 square feet. Mack's boasted ornate window displays at Christmas and at one time was the premier destination of the Main Street shopping district.

Fire broke out at the Mack & Company store on May 15, 1899, in the third-floor upholsterers' room. The *Ann Arbor Argus-Democrat* reported that the cause was unknown but possibly was a result of "combustion" or the sun's refraction on cotton and oils. News reports at the time said that if the wind had been blowing in a different direction, the fire could have spread up Main Street. Fortunately, two Good Samaritans, Charlie Thomas and "Shorty Foot Ball" Allen, helped put out the fire. It was reported that thousands of spectators applauded the two for their heroics and bravery.

Mack, who bought out his partner Schmid's interest in 1895, later passed his store to his son, Walter, who had begun working for his dad in 1884. Unfortunately, it did not survive the Great Depression and closed in the late 1930s. In 1940, the Cunningham Drugstore chain took over part of the Mack & Company location. The drugstore featured green panels that were eventually removed as businesses and owners changed hands. In 2012, the Lena restaurant moved in and included "Cunningham green" panels, which lasted as long as Lena did (until 2016).

William Goodyear and Bruno St. James came to town in 1888 to open a dry goods store. They only had $1,200 capital (about $31,000 today), and skeptics were everywhere. But Goodyear had started working in dry goods in Detroit when he was just twelve years old and knew the business. Located at 122 South Main Street (5 Main Street back then), Goodyear & St. James soon became a staple of downtown. In 1895, Goodyear bought out St. James and moved next door to 118 Main Street. St. James stayed and opened his own store in the space that would later house Muehlig's. (Fortunately, the break did not appear to extend into their personal lives, as William Goodyear married Bruno St. James's sister Delia.) The little business kept on growing. In 1902, Goodyear bought E.F. Mills & Company and took over its space. He incorporated in 1916; at that time, Paul Proud (who had married St. James's daughter) took over as president of the corporation, a position he held until 1961. Goodyear's saw some other expansions in 1949, when it took over the Woolworth building, and then nine years later, when it took over the Muir Drugstore. The store also opened a location at 213 South State Street in 1950 that included a restaurant; that location closed in 1958. Locals knew Goodyear's for many things—free gift wrapping, free delivery and attentive customer service. When it celebrated its ninetieth anniversary in 1978, it brought in over $2.5 million in annual revenue. At that time, the *Ann Arbor News* described it as going from "being operated by a couple of men to…managed and operated almost totally by women."

Kline's, located at 306 South Main Street, opened in 1930 and specialized in mass-produced goods that were less expensive. Known for having continuous sales, Kline's directly competed with stores like Mack &

Goodyear and St. James. *Bentley Historical Library.*

Mack & Company. *Bentley Historical Library.*

Company. In 1940, Sears built a store right next to Kline's, which moved into the space when Sears left for Briarwood Mall. Kline's closed in 1994, and within a few years, the Ark moved to Kline's second-floor space.

Near Kline's was Hutzel's Ladies Wear at 301 South Main Street (later home to the Selo/Shevel gallery and now Shinola). Established by Charles Hutzel in 1916, the shop expanded several times, taking over the Kellogg Corset shop (by simply removing a wall partition) and the Francisco and Boyle Photo Company.

Hutzel came to Ann Arbor as a child and began working in the city when he was sixteen. After working in Mack & Company's ready-to-wear department, he spent some time in Battle Creek before coming home to open his own store. On the day of Hutzel's grand opening, Walter Mack sent all of his customers over to shop, and another department store owner named Eugene Mills took out an ad in the paper to welcome to new business. Charles passed away in 1943 at the age of sixty-six; his son Raymond Hutzel sold the business out of the family in 1969.

When Fred Wuerth asked Albert Fiegel to buy his business in the early 1920s, neither could have foreseen the decades of success that would ensue. Fiegel grew up on a farm in Pittsfield Township and was educated in a one-

Kline's. *Bentley Historical Library.*

room schoolhouse. He originally planned to become a minister, but after his father's untimely and tragic death, he had to abandon those plans. In 1891, at the age of eighteen, Fiegel went to work for what was then named Wadhams, Ryan & Reule at the corner of Main and Washington Streets. He did well enough to buy in as a partner and change the name of the store; as of 1916, it became known as Reule, Conlin & Fiegel Company.

Reule, Conlin & Fiegel. *Bentley Historical Library.*

Working in the old building hurt Fiegel's health to the extent that his doctor advised him to quit his job. After a time of recuperation, Fiegel began working at Mack's Department Store. It was there in the early 1920s that Fred Wuerth approached Fiegel about buying his menswear business at 322–324 South Main Street. Fiegel bought Wuerth's business in 1927 and renamed it after himself, adding "since 1891," which was the year Fiegel entered the world of clothes selling, not the actual year that the business was founded. The business ran successfully for years; in 1941, employees Herb Sager, John Andress and Paul Jedele became the new owners of the business. They initially put up a sign bearing their names but quickly returned to Fiegel's after seeing a noticeable drop in sales. In 1965, they gained 60 percent more floor space by moving next door to the space formerly occupied by the Wuerth Theater. (Apollo Music took the original Fiegel's spot.)

Albert Fiegel enjoyed a nice life, marrying a woman named Hannah and having a daughter named Gertrude. He passed away in the 1940s, but his store operated as Fiegel's Men's and Boys' Wear into the 1990s. An interesting footnote is the Centennial Award granted to the business in 1991. As noted above, Fiegel's sign indicated the year he entered the clothes selling business, not the actual date his own store began operations. But someone read the sign, did the math and gave out the award! Regardless of the actual date, Fiegel's store enjoyed a long and fruitful life.

While many residents are beloved to Ann Arbor, Bertha Muehlig holds a very special place in the hearts of many people. The story begins when Philip Bach replaced an old wooden storefront at Main and Washington Streets with a new building around 1865 (now the home of the Hooper Hathaway law offices). Bach went into business with Peter Abel, Eugene Abel and Zachary Roath, ultimately spending almost thirty years in the dry goods business. In 1891, he hired a young woman named Bertha Muehlig to be the business's bookkeeper.

Just a few months before his death in 1895, Bach sold his store to Bruno St. James, who was at the time co-owner of Goodyear & St. James. By that time, Muehlig was twenty-one years old, had been working at the business for four years and continued her employment with the new management. When St. James passed away sixteen years later, Muehlig bought the business, changed the name, and worked in the store for decades. Muehlig's is fondly remembered as selling everything a housewife could need—aprons, dresses, handkerchiefs, baby supplies and purses—packed into the three floors of the storefront.

Muehlig spent her life in a home at 315 South Main Street, just a block and a half away from her business. She was known as a generous person, giving to local charities, hospitals and churches, and was ultimately dubbed the "Santa Claus of Ann Arbor." When Muehlig passed away at the age of eighty-one, she left her store to two of her employees and a nephew. The business carried on until 1980, but the memories of Muehlig's attentive personal care, outstanding customer service and generosity will live on in the hearts of locals who remember.

Like many other towns, Ann Arbor's downtown was home to bigger chains, such as Kresge (where BD's Mongolian Grill is now) and Jacobson's (in the same building where Borders eventually ended its run). Many chains dotted the landscape in larger shopping centers, such as Toys R Us, Burlington Coat Factory, Linens 'n Things, Musicland, Radio Shack, F&M, Pier One, Service Merchandise, American Bulk Food and several Kmart locations.

Other Retail Highlights

Tally Hall, a two-story mall and marketplace beneath a six-story parking lot that included a food court, marked the first time the city's public and private sectors joined for a commercial development. Located between Washington and Liberty Streets and near Division Street, the mall struggled to attract tenants and shoppers and now is home to a variety of private and university offices. The parking structure remains operational.

At one time, many bakeries flourished in Ann Arbor, including Dough Boys Bakery, Lunsford's Bakery, Sun Bakery, Maser's Bakery, Hansen's Bakery, Deluxe Bakery and Pastry Shop, Creamo Bakery, Jacques Patisserie, Campbell Bakery, Gauss Bakery and the recently closed Pastry Peddler.

When townies talk about bakeries that are very much missed, almost inevitably the Quality Bakery is mentioned. Oscar Laubengayer and Ferdinand Drebes opened the bakery on Main Street in 1920. After Drebes passed away in 1949, Laubengayer ran the business until his death in 1964, weathering a fire in 1955 that burned both the bakery and its neighbor, the Modern Appliance. Ten years after Laubengayer's passing, his daughter Betty Lutz and her husband, Burt, began daily operations. Specialties included sour cream donuts, pretzels, Long Johns and pecan rolls. Customers could buy at the bakery or at places around town, such as Drake's. When Quality Bakery closed its doors in 1987, it employed twenty people and fed its homemade goods to countless more.

Other stores that hopefully inspire memories include Ehnis and Sons (a clothing store on West Liberty Street), Seyfried Jewelers, Haller Jewelry Store, Haarer and Goetz, Grand Illusion Gallery (coauthor Woodman remembers the store as filled with the edges of pop art such as pinup illustrations and adult film one-sheet posters, from a time when adult films were exhibited in theaters), the South U Galleria (now a Starbucks, a post office and University of Michigan offices), Hirth Brothers' Dairy, Betsy Ross in Nickels Arcade, Safer Sex Store, Wizzywigs, Stein & Goetz (a sports shop on Main Street), Bead Bag, Bead Gallery, Fox Tent & Awning, Frank's Nursery and Trim, Bavarian Village Ski Shop, Artisans, John Leidy (which had a huge sale every November), Antique Village, Evangeline's Second Notice, Fantasy Fashions, Good Pickin's, Kay's Klothes Kloset, Ozzie's, Ragtop Vintage Clothing, Beer Vault (a drive-through beer store), Second Hand Rose, Woman in the Shoe, Little Things, Marti Walker, Kay Baum, Paraphernalia (a dress shop on State Street in the late 1960s), Stangers, Leslie Office Supply, Schlenker

Hardware, the Tree (a consignment shop), Fantasy Attic (costume shop), Learning Ladder, the Magic Shoppe, Needle Beedle Beads and Craft Supplies, Delahats Tots to Teens, Little Boot Shop, Russell's Women's Apparel, Wilkinson's (a luggage store), Kitchen Port, Felicia Brothers Shoes, Frank Tice's Men's Shop, Dick Kay's Marathon, Shipman's Toy Store, the Skate Exchange, the Needlepoint Tree, Middle Earth, Ryder's Hobby Shop, Campus Bike & Toy, Kiddie Land, Peaceable Kingdom, Falling Water, Wild's Menswear, Faber's Fabrics, Mayer Schairer & Company, Merchant of Vino, the Bagpiper, Video Watch (later acquired by Hollywood Video), Liberty Street Video, Campus Video and Harry's Army Surplus (originally at Fourth Avenue and Washington Street and later at Liberty and Thompson Streets, where Douglas J Salon is now).

Record stores of the past included Schoolkids Records, SKR Classical (the space was also briefly SKR Rock and SKR Jazz), Schoolkids in Exile, Apollo Music, Record Bar/TRACKS Music & Video, Tower Records (which at first only took up eight thousand square feet but later expanded to the entire second floor to offer more video and books), Michigan Wherehouse Records,

Middle Earth. *Bentley Historical Library.*

Left: Harry's Army Surplus when it was on Fourth Avenue and Washington Street. *Bentley Historical Library.*

Below: Wazoo record store in 1976. *Bentley Historical Library.*

Play It Again Records, Music-Go-Round/Record Exchange, State Discount (a variety store that had locations on several Midwest college campuses including Michigan State and the University of Wisconsin–Madison) and Al Nalli's Music.

5

CITY SERVICES

From Fire Prevention to Waterworks

Court

As Ann Arbor grew from small town to larger town to small city, so did its government and transportation services. Upon the town's founding, Rumsey set aside half a square block on Liberty Street (between Fourth and Fifth Avenues) to be used as a county jail; today, that area is home to our federal courthouse and post office. For his part, Allen donated a square block of land surrounded by Huron Street, Main Street, Fourth Avenue and Ann Street to be used as a public courthouse and square; not surprisingly, that area became known as Courthouse Square. That square became the heart of the small community. Soldiers set off for active duty, politicians delivered speeches that they hoped would lead to their election, parades launched, and citizens gathered to hear about President Lincoln's assassination. People posed for photographs with their bicycle club, with their friends and family or by themselves. Children played, people gossiped, families picnicked, and bands played. It is not an exaggeration to call this area the heart of Ann Arbor for at least a hundred years.

Our first courthouse—and the first courthouse in the county—was built on Ann Street in the square in 1834 for about $5,000. The two-story brick building featured an upstairs courtroom and cupola. Downstairs, lawyers rented office space. Outside, a white fence and many hitching posts surrounded Courthouse Square.

Our first courthouse was located on Ann Street in the Courthouse Square. *Bentley Historical Library.*

Our burgeoning town began to outgrow its modest courthouse, and the voters were asked to approve the building of a new one in 1866. The voters turned this down but approved a new building just eleven years later. According to Grace Shackman's 1990 article for the *Observer*, this approval may have in part been due to a fire that struck the office of the sheriff. A fire like that could have destroyed every single court record since the beginning of the town.

Thanks to that approval of funds, builders constructed an extravagant courthouse in the center of the square. Under the shade of nearby trees, the three-story redbrick building stood proudly, boasting a seven-story clock tower and smaller towers at the corners with statues of justice perched above the entrances. Built for a total of about $88,000, this courthouse served its residents for almost eighty years.

Other city business needs also had to be addressed, and as city services increased, so did the need for space. In 1895, city leaders rented space in the city building on Fourth Avenue. Finally, in 1907, our first city hall was completed.

ATTENTION!
INDIGNATION MEETING

The Citizens of Ann Arbor, are requested to meet at the Court House this evening, at 6 o'clock, to take into consideration the conduct of the *FACULTY* of the University of Michigan, in *Expelling* all the Students belonging to Secret Societies!

December 20, 1849. **MANY CITIZENS.**

Indignation Meeting at the Courthouse Square! *Bentley Historical Library.*

Our beautiful, majestic courthouse. *Bentley Historical Library.*

Ann Arbor's first city hall, at the corner of Fifth Avenue and Huron Street, was finished in 1907. *Bentley Historical Library.*

In 1834, John Allen served as our village president. When Ann Arbor was incorporated into a city in 1851, those who were legally able to vote began electing mayors and councilmembers. Originally called the common council, this body has been meeting in Ann Arbor for over 150 years. Folks in Ann Arbor celebrated their new status as a city by gathering at the train depot to welcome back George Sedgwick, the man credited as the force behind the passage of the exciting law. The crowd cheered, the band played, and the men later elected Sedgwick as mayor. Two days after that election, the first council meeting was held. Since then, the representatives of our city's wards meet two to three times a month to address issues such as street repair, disorderly persons, electric lights and eventually modern problems of zoning, deer overpopulation and annexation of land.

POST OFFICE

Our exquisite post office stood at the northeast corner of Main and Ann Streets, offering both the mail and social opportunities. Because home delivery of daily mail had not yet been introduced to our city, people had to trek down to the post office to get their packages and letters. It was not only a place for gossip but was also considered a "respectable" meeting spot for men and women. After home delivery began in 1886, the building lost some of its luster as a social spot, and a new building was used after the turn of the century. This gorgeous building was demolished in 1940.

By 1950, home mail delivery had been around in Ann Arbor for almost seventy years. It was no big deal to see mail carriers with their bags of letters. But maybe it was a bigger deal for the people who saw a yellow cocker spaniel named Dusty as he accompanied postal carriers on their appointed rounds. Dusty lived with his owner, Diane Ottosen, on North Main Street and began making the rounds with carrier Kenny Friskey. After Friskey moved away in 1953, Dusty met carrier C.H. "Jack" Crippen on his route, and the routine began again. Dusty followed Crippen along his four-and-a-half-mile route around the North Main Street area, into the post office, and would have followed him home if Crippen did not bring

5438. U. S. Post Office, Ann Arbor, Mich.

Second post office, at 220 North Main Street. *Bentley Historical Library.*

him to the Ottosen home after the shift ended. Crippen told the *Ann Arbor News* that he once tried to sneak out of the back of a building, only to have Dusty catch up to him a few steps later.

Libraries

Just three years after Allen and Rumsey founded our fair city in 1824, a group called the Ann Arbor Library Association began meeting. This was not a public library as we know it; it relied upon the dues paid by patrons. Using the dues it collected, the association purchased one hundred books by 1830.

Around the same time, the Ann Arbor Circulating Library sprang up at the office of the *Western Emigrant* (the first newspaper in Ann Arbor). Dues were $2.50 per year and were mainly used to purchase reference books. The following decade produced another Ann Arbor Library Association and the Working Men's Library Association. Like that very first group, these were not funded by taxes but by private dues and donations. However, government-sponsored public libraries were coming soon.

In 1843, the state school superintendent decreed that all school districts had to set up their own libraries, earmark at least twenty-five dollars for the collections and share the books with local townships. Since these were to be public, non-dues-paying organizations, the state government announced two years later that various collected fines by local government units would go to the libraries. (The only exception was in cases where the monies were instead needed for the local poorhouse.)

Our local school district began purchasing books as early as March 1844, as reported by the *Michigan State Journal*. Twelve years later, in 1856, the Ann Arbor School District's library books were consolidated into a space in the first public high school, the Union School on State Street between Washington and Huron Streets. Because this new space was open to the public, 1856 is the date generally given as the beginning of the public library system in Ann Arbor.

In 1877, the *Michigan Argus* reported that a teacher at the school was charged with the school district library's keeping. At that time, around 600 books were available, about 250 of which were checked out at any given time. Teachers kept the library open once a week while school was in session except when they closed it to "call in the books." In 1876, an average of 48.6 books were lent each week, with a high of 92 books lent during the last week of the year. Scott, Dickens and Hawthorne were almost always checked out, as were travel books and books of essays. No taxes were levied for the library, nor were general school funds used—the only money used for the acquisition of new books came from the "small quota" of fines that came through the county treasurer, as per the state requirement discussed above. Apparently, it was not much, because the *Michigan Argus* rather sarcastically noted that our county was either full of law-abiding citizens or else didn't impose or collect fines like other counties, because the funds just weren't making their way to the library. The paper advocated that more money should be made available so that the holdings could be increased and the library open one full afternoon and one full evening at least once per week for the entire year.

The following year, the *Michigan Argus* printed the report of our local superintendent. He described the library as being "well selected [and] well patronized" but too small. Only $59.60 worth of fines were received the prior year, so he asked the school board to appropriate $100 per year to enlarge the collection and allow it to "finally become a credit to the city."

Finances must have improved for the school district library, as it hired Nellie Loving to supervise its collection of books in 1883. Her first task was overseeing the move of the two-thousand-book collection from the superintendent's office to a space on the second floor. Loving spent almost forty years working in our library system, becoming a beloved librarian and the namesake of the Loving Branch (replaced by the Malletts Creek Branch in 2004).

An *Ann Arbor Courier* article from 1886 announced "good reading free!" at the library, which had grown to 2,500 books with "almost an entire absence of what is known as 'trash.' " There were some rules to be followed: one had to be at least fourteen years old to check out a book, only one book could be checked out at a time, and one could not lend it to someone else. There was a two-week maximum check out time, with a ten-cent-per-week fee if a book was not returned on time, and one was liable for damages if the book was harmed while under one's care. On regular schooldays, patrons could check out a book from 8:30 a.m. until 1:00 p.m., and while students were the primary consumers, the "good natured librarian" would attend to calls "at any time." The general public could come by on Wednesday from 4:00 to 5:00 p.m. Loving reported that there were 10,000 checkouts per year, which may have accounted for the "well worn and discolored" books.

Carnegie Library, 700 East Huron Street near State Street, 1938. *Bentley Historical Library.*

By this time, the library was funded by fines, dog tax money and appropriations at annual school meetings. The *Courier* called for "some scheme" to be invented to produce a permanent fund for the library.

In 1889, builders completed an addition to the school that included a room set aside for the library. In 1904, during the time that the board of education was working to put a Carnegie library next to the high school, both the school and the library room burned down. Fortunately, most of the library's holdings (by then over eight thousand books) were saved. In 1905, Carnegie guaranteed the funds, and voters later approved a bond for a new school. When the buildings reopened in 1906, they were connected by a passageway and fireproof door.

Schools

Just a year after the founding of Ann Arbor, John Allen built a log-cabin school on his property at the northwest corner of Main and Ann Streets. Miss Monroe taught at the primary school, which historical accounts describe as a "crude building" with small glass windows and split-log benches.

In those early days, public funds did not support schools as they do today. Instead, rate bills and other assessments were levied on parents whose children attended the school (public schools were not authorized until 1830, and it wasn't until years later that tax money supported education efforts). Many of the local school-aged boys and girls did not attend school—in 1832, out of 161 possible pupils aged five to fifteen, only 35 were enrolled in school. By 1838, that number had increased to 70, still far below the total number of age-appropriate children.

Secondary education options included a variety of private schools, including the Merrill brothers' school, which was founded in 1829 and described by local media as "a select school...for teaching higher English and Latin and Greek," or the Misses Clark's School.

One of the most successful and prosperous private schools, the Misses Clark's Seminary for Young Ladies was started in 1839 by the three Clark sisters, wealthy and well-educated women from New York. Affluent parents from near and far sent their daughters to the school. Mary Clark, who served as principal, ensured instruction not only in morals but also in nature. A botanist, she saw to it that her female pupils received an education in the observations of the natural world by taking them on

Clark Girls School at 505 North Division Street. *Ann Arbor District Library.*

Right: Mary Clark. *Ann Arbor District Library.*

Below: Ann Arbor High School pre-1905. *Bentley Historical Library.*

weekly hikes to collect and study wildflowers. The Clark sisters did not allow their students to have "callers" except on weekends and only if Mary was present. They operated the school until Mary's death in 1875. The school's final location was 505 North Division Street; the building has since been converted into apartments.

THE ANN ARBOR HIGH SCHOOL, 1907

Ann Arbor High School, 1907. *Bentley Historical Library.*

The first true public school, Ann Arbor's Union School, opened on October 5, 1856. Known as the Union High School and located on State Street between Huron and Washington Streets, it housed students of all ages until the elementary grades moved out in the 1860s. After the departure of the younger students, the school became known as Ann Arbor High School.

Each ward in the city had its own primary school: Ward One's school, constructed in 1862 and later purchased by the University of Michigan and renamed West Hall, was located near where the Betsy Barbour Residence hall is today; Ward Two's school was at Bach (which remains an elementary school); Ward Three's was the Mack School, which remains in operation today as the Ann Arbor Open School at Mack; Ward Four's was the building that later housed Jones School and now is home to Community High School; and Ward Five's school (later called the Donovan School) was located on Wall Street around where the Kellogg Eye Center is today.

In 1904, Ann Arbor High School burned down; the rebuilt school opened in 1906 at the corner of State and Huron Streets (later the Frieze Building). In 1956, a brand-new Ann Arbor High School opened at the corner of Stadium Boulevard and South Main Street. When Huron High School opened in 1967 at Huron Parkway and Fuller Road, Ann Arbor High School was renamed Pioneer High School.

A Glimpse into Graduating Classes of the Past

Ann Arbor High School's class of 1872 graduated with prayer and lots of lovely music. Interestingly, students were able to pick different courses to guide their studies: classical, Latin, English, scientific, English/French, English/German, German/French, English/scientific, German or French. Beloved Professor Walter Perry even came back and received a cane from his former students.

The June 22, 1887 issue of the *Courier* reported that classes were scheduled to be completed that day and that seniors were enjoying themselves at Whitmore Lake. A month earlier, the seniors had "class day" at Whitmore Lake, wherein they held mock classes imitating the ones held at the school for the previous sixteen years. To make the high school "show up well for commencement," electric lights were put up in some of the rooms.

In 1894, eighty-six students graduated from Ann Arbor High School. The *Argus* warned the graduates that while they might take a "roseate" view of the future, they would not find "everything just as they expected." Indeed, a man's shirt collar was sure to melt down as he pulled the ragweed from himself and suffered blisters on his hands. A woman's hands were sure to be reddened with the "host dish-washer of post-graduation" life. That, advised the newspaper, is why this is called commencement—because it is the beginning of real, practical life. Despite these ominous warnings, the class of '94 still managed to have a nice celebration, decorating the graduation hall in the class colors, pink and blue. Speeches were made, diplomas were handed out, and the orchestra played the "Cocoanut Dance." This dance got people standing up and swaying in a "rhythmic movement." Even some of the deacons joined in!

Ann Arbor High School's class of 1898 celebrated graduation on July 1. The class colors, black and gold, adorned the stage where fifty-nine students received their diplomas. School colors of corn and maroon festooned the rest of the hall. After an opening prayer, the high school orchestra performed. Principal Judson Pattengill handed out the diplomas and was followed by several class speakers who presented their essays on topics ranging from "Problems of Great Cities" to "The Romance of the Sea."

WATER

Our founders settled near two bodies of water—the Huron River and what was later named Allen's Creek. This surely was not an accident. They needed water for drinking, bathing, cooking and trading.

The first public wells were constructed in the 1840s, beginning at the south side of the courthouse and various street intersections. Maynard and Liberty Street boasted a well with stone walls that was ninety feet deep. Families paid one dollar each year for the privilege of using its water. Corner pumps began to be installed, and they proved to be great temptations for the pranks of high school students. The superintendent declared "pumping" a misdemeanor punishable by suspension.

In the 1860s, when the city was young, a private company named the Artesian Well Company provided water. After its demise, the city authorized another private company called the Ann Arbor Water Company to build a waterworks system. The station pumped water from the Huron River to the reservoir on Sunset Road, and then pipes carried the water down into the city.

Fire was always a concern of early settlements. In response to this, large cisterns and wells were dug by the city. In 1886, the private water company installed over one hundred fire hydrants and guaranteed water pressure sufficient to combat fires. By 1897, it installed more hydrants and opened up an auxiliary station on West Washington Street. This was possibly in response to the concerns raised by the mayor in 1894—specifically, that the private water company had breached its contract with the city and was guilty of criminal negligence. These charges were made when the city's fire chief was informed that the hydrant pressures were not sufficient for fire protection. Three years later, the fire chief stated to the common council that he anticipated no more trouble thanks to the additional pipes and hydrants installed by the Ann Arbor Water Company.

Of course, drinking water was also of paramount importance for the growing city. Initially, steam-powered pumps were used to obtain water from artesian wells that had been dug around the city. More and more people came to the city, and the wells were unable to keep up with demand. Thus, in 1900, the Huron River became a source for water. That same year, the city installed a filter bed to remove the sediment that collected in the water. At its September 15, 1913 meeting, the common council proposed to purchase the Ann Arbor Water Company for $450,000. Our water has been under the control of the city ever since.

Waterworks. *Bentley Historical Library.*

Our current water treatment plant on Sunset Road was built in 1938. Additions were made to it in 1945. A second plant was built in 1966 and added onto in 1975. Between the two, they process fifty million gallons of water per day. The folks who work at these plants constantly monitor our water, keeping it potable for us.

Water from the Huron River is still used and accounts for about 85 percent of the water we use; the remaining water comes from wells. Primarily, the treatment plant uses ozone and chloramines (a combined chlorine mixture) to disinfect the water. The latter disinfectant has fewer byproducts and less odor and taste than chlorine. The water is softened with calcium hydroxide, fluoride is added, the water is filtered and disinfected—and just like that, we have safe water coming from the taps in our homes.

In 1906, the common council said words that are still true today: "There is no more important interest in a community than its water supply."

FIRE

Early Ann Arborites had reason to worry about the threat of fire; it was a constant danger, as the town's buildings and the sidewalks in front of them were all wood. Thus, just twelve years after the village's founding, Ann Arbor's Ordinance Relating to a Fire Department passed. Approved on December 12, 1836, the ordinance ran seven pages long and appointed fire wardens and volunteer fire companies in the town's two wards. Nine years later, a code of fire rules was adopted that stated, "Upon hearing the cry of fire, every citizen, under 'pain of punishment' must call 'fire' at the top of his lungs and go to the scene with a bucket or pail." In 1854, the fire companies joined together as a unified unit known as the Fire Department of the City of Ann Arbor.

A small, two-story, wooden firemen's hall was constructed but eventually proved insufficient to meet the needs of the growing town. The volunteer

It is believed that the term "first call" was unique to our first department. The, term, created in the 1800s, meant that the engine and ladder company in the front of the station responded, while a "second call" meant that the fire equipment in the back of the station would be used. *Bentley Historical Library.*

firemen lobbied successfully for a new firemen's hall, and the result was a hall that at the time was the most elegant and expensive city-owned building. Opening in 1882, the new hall had a second floor for meetings and social events, a first floor to store hooks and ladders and a bell tower to summon the volunteer firefighters. While that majestic building adequately housed the men, horses and equipment, the fire company had to rely on stored rainwater for fighting fires until 1885, when one hundred fire hydrants were installed.

The men served as unpaid volunteers until 1888, when the city hired the first paid firefighters. A year later, the common council approved a sixty-day trial of a professional department, authorizing the hiring of three men and purchase of one hose wagon and one team of horses. The horses had second jobs—they plowed city land when not pulling equipment to fires. The building would house our fire department for ninety-six years and is now home to the Ann Arbor Hands-On Museum. Meanwhile, the department moved to a new building just north of this one.

BURIAL

The first public burial ground of non-Natives was located at what is now Felch Park, next to the Power Center for Performing Arts. Early maps show designated land for a "private cemetery" just to the west of this location; one corner of this area was marked as the "Hebrew Burial ground." In 1843, a resolution "for improving and ornamenting the public Burying Ground of this village" was passed, leading to the planting of trees at the site. In 1891, the city converted the cemetery into a park honoring former governor Alpheus Felch. The bodies were reinterred in Fairview Cemetery in Lower Town.

TRANSPORTATION

The arrival of the train in Ann Arbor was the first step toward faster travel times to new locations. The first printed mention of a transcontinental railroad appeared in the *Western Emigrant* of Ann Arbor in 1832. Later that year, the Detroit & St. Joseph Railroad was chartered, planning a railway

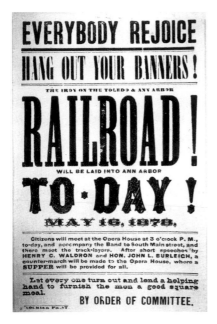

EVERYBODY REJOICE

HANG OUT YOUR BANNERS!

THE IRON ON THE TOLEDO & ANN ARBOR

RAILROAD!

WILL BE LAID INTO ANN ARBOR

TO·DAY!

MAY 16, 1878.

Citizens will meet at the Opera House at 3 o'clock P. M., to-day, and accompany the Band to South Main street, and there meet the track-layers. After short speeches by HENRY C. WALDRON and HON. JOHN L. BURLEIGH, a countermarch will be made to the Opera House, where a SUPPER will be provided for all.

Let every one turn out and lend a helping hand to furnish the men a good square meal.

BY ORDER OF COMMITTEE.

Headline announcing the railroad—everybody rejoice! *Bentley Historical Library.*

that would span our state. In 1833, the Erie & Kalamazoo Railroad laid the first tracks in Michigan, between Adrian and Toledo. Three years later, the railroad company went to Detroit and began laying track headed west. The trains reached Ypsilanti by 1838 and Ann Arbor in October 1839. A train trip from Detroit to Ann Arbor took about two and a half hours, compared to an entire day by horse and buggy.

The Michigan Central Railroad incorporated in 1846, and six years later, the tracks reached Chicago. The first depot in Ann Arbor was built in 1845 but is lost to history. Fortunately, the one built forty-one years later continues to delight passersby today.

In 1886, architect Frederick Spiers collaborated with William C. Rohn to build the beautiful structure at 401 Depot Street. The Richardsonian Romanesque style the men used has been described as incorporating styles of eleventh- and twelfth-century France. The elegant depot used stones quarried at Four Mile Lake in Chelsea and was called by the *Ann Arbor Register* "the finest station...between Buffalo and Chicago." Pictures and written descriptions from the era confirm this compliment. Inside the depot, travelers walked on French tile floors. They looked up at stained-glass windows and red oak ceilings. Outside, people enjoyed flower gardens and a fountain.

Today, part of the Ann Arbor Railroad is owned by the state, and part of the rails are owned by a private company. Amtrak uses the former Michigan Central route as part of its east–west line, running the Wolverine passenger train three times each day. Built in 1983, the Amtrak station sits just to the west of the original depot and recently had a major upgrade when a platform compliant with the Americans with Disabilities Act was added.

The Michigan Central Railroad ran without competition until 1878, when the Toledo & Ann Arbor Railroad, familiarly called the "Annie," began serving the city. A joyous announcement in the *Courier* urged citizens to meet at the opera house at 3:00 p.m., accompany the city band to meet

The Ann Arbor Railroad depot on Ashley Street in 1912. *Bentley Historical Library.*

the track layers and then march back to the opera house for a dinner. A small train depot was built at 416 South Ashley Street.

Ann Arbor can thank that street's namesake, James "Big Jim" Ashley, for this north–south railway, which reached the city on May 16, 1878. After that, Ashley kept building the line in the northwest direction. Ultimately, the tracks led to Frankfort, then known for its harbor service.

Ann Arbor residents enjoyed taking the Annie up to Whitmore Lake for dancing or sunbathing. Passenger service increased in the summer months and again in the fall, when people from all over the Midwest attended University of Michigan football games. The summer traffic was so heavy that eight trains a day ran between Ann Arbor and Whitmore Lake; the run was nicknamed the "Ping Pong Special." Passenger service continued until 1950.

WHO WAS BIG JIM ASHLEY?

So, who was "Big Jim"? Well, there were actually two James Ashleys—father and son. The elder Ashley was a special friend of Abraham Lincoln and had the idea to create a railroad link between Toledo and Ann Arbor. According to Wikipedia, the senior James Ashley was born in 1824, but an 1899 *New*

York Times article puts Ashley at the age of sixty in 1877, which would mean his birth was in 1817. In that same article, James Ashley Sr. is also referred to as "Old Jim" or the "Governor," as he was named governor of the Montana Territory when military governors were appointed after the Civil War. By most accounts, James was a good and honest man who abhorred slavery and sought to be fair in his work.

Ashley's eldest son was born in 1853, also named James and called Jim. An 1899 *New York Times* article reported that this Jim stood six feet, five inches, and had the "strength of two ordinary men."

Despite the large stature of Jim Jr., most local historical records refer to James Sr. as "Big Jim," the one who built the railroad and after whom the street is named. Whether he actually laid track is not clear, but he is reported to have initially had the idea for the Ann Arbor Railroad. Despite his position and special relationship with Lincoln, the financial panic of the 1870s left James Sr. nearly bankrupt and looking for a new life plan.

By happenstance, James Sr. met T.A. Scott, the former master of transportation during the Civil War. Scott liked his railroad plan and helped him secure rails and materials. James Sr. financed construction primarily on credit and quickly got into deep debt as his group secured the road from Toledo to Ann Arbor with the intent to extend rails all the way up to Mount Pleasant. Adding to James Sr.'s troubles were legal issues over the crossing of Michigan Central tracks near Howell.

In 1877, the Michigan Central Railroad company lobbied to get Michigan's "crossing laws" (which allowed one railroad to cross over the tracks of another) repealed. By this point, any delay in James Sr.'s dream would doom the entire operation. In fact, $200,000 in investment required that the tracks near Howell be completed. If they were not laid, the money would not be paid.

As the track layers reached the point of crossing and were stopped by Michigan Central, it looked like Jim Sr. could go no further—that is, until his eldest son, Jim Jr., got involved. Even though he was only twenty-five years old, Jim Jr. understood the gravity of the situation and took action—he formed a small army to get the railroad built over the Michigan Central tracks.

Jim Jr. gathered 200 of his closest daredevil friends, armed them and prepared to lay some track. And just in case, he sent for 250 more men from the toughest part of Toledo. Carrying muskets and bayonets, the men converged near Howell on December 26, 1878. Jim Jr.'s plan was to simply dig a tunnel under the Michigan Central tracks for his Ann Arbor tracks.

During a cold winter night, using dynamite and his hand-crafted army, Jim Jr. oversaw the track construction of the Ann Arbor Railroad.

As one might guess, Michigan Central was not happy about this turn of events and sent in its workmen to tear up what Jim Jr. had built. By midnight of that very same day, Jim Jr. returned with his men. A few shots were fired, much macho behavior was no doubt displayed, and the Michigan Central folks backed down, jumped into waiting train cars and retreated down the track. Jim Jr.'s men then tore up the Michigan Central tracks, took some of their rails and blasted out a new tunnel.

The next four days brought various writs from the court, all of which Jim Jr. declined to follow. A friendlier judge issued his own writs, spawning what the *New York Times* called a "siege." Jim Jr. and his men stood in the "bitterest cold and deepest snow known…to that cold party of the country" for twelve days. Sympathetic local farmers brought the men food and hot coffee. The siege finally ended when the governor, railroad commissioner and a U.S. marshal showed up to order that trains were to run on both roads until a court could properly decide the matter. They then promptly arrested Jim Jr. for obstruction. He ended up serving no jail time but was fined $102.50 and costs by a Detroit judge.

So, where was James "Big Jim" Sr. all of this time? In New York, overseeing financial issues related to the building of the railway. It appears that James Sr. took care of the money end, but it was Jim Jr. whose boots were on the ground as the tracks got laid.

In 1890, James Sr. fell ill, and he eventually died in Alma, Michigan, six years later. Jim Jr. fell on hard financial times after the completion of the railroad and ended up moving south. He landed in Georgia, where he rebuilt his wealth by promoting power plants and trading in lumber. He ran for Congress twice but, unlike his father, was not successful. He passed away after a heart attack in 1919.

Trolleys

In the summer of 1890, workers laid the first streetcar track in our city. The system was initially designed to be powered by horses but was switched to electric power a few months before cars began running in 1891.

The first line ran from Ann Arbor to Ypsilanti down Packard Street. Later, the Depot Line ran from the railroad station to downtown, east on William

A trolley chugs down Main Street past Mack & Company in this undated photograph. *Bentley Historical Library.*

A trolley with the courthouse in the background. Note the spelling of "base ball" on the trolley advertisement. *Ann Arbor District Library.*

Posing with the local streetcar on Packard Street are its motorman, Jim Love, and the conductor, Marion Darling. At times, the motorman would call out, "Ready, Darling?" and the conductor would reply, "Yes, Love." *Bentley Historical Library.*

Street, branching off into a north-and-south route at State Street. Riders could go up North University Avenue to Washtenaw Avenue to Hill Street or south on Monroe Street to East University Avenue to Hill Street. A second route went from Veterans' Park on the westside to downtown, continuing southeast on Packard Street.

By 1900, there were six and a half miles of track and ten trolleys. Just twenty-five years later, buses took over; the last run for the streetcars was on January 30, 1925. Interurbans ran until 1929, leaving only the tracks that they and the trolleys used. Those tracks were removed by WPA work crews during the Great Depression. Occasionally, street work or poor weather unearths remnants of the old tracks.

RECENT FAREWELLS

The saying goes that you're either changing or you're dying. If that is true, then Ann Arbor is very far from its deathbed. Since the beginning of the writing of this book, numerous local businesses have closed their doors. While they have vanished from our city's landscape, we hope they are not soon forgotten. In addition to the entities listed below, the following businesses closed in 2018: Edward Brothers Malloy publishers, Moe Sports Shops, the Bead Gallery and Adorn Me.

Robin and Jamie Agnew opened Aunt Agatha's—a play on the name of a Minneapolis bookstore called Uncle Edgar's—in 1992. Over the years, the couple sold countless mystery tomes, often guiding readers to just the right book. The store supported many authors, especially local writers, frequently sponsoring book signings and special events.

Vogel's Lock and Safe, at 113 West Washington Street, opened in 1913 and closed in March 2018. When Gus Vogel Sr. bought the building, it belonged to the Lutz family and operated as a machine shop. For over one hundred years, the Vogel family rekeyed businesses, repaired locks and safes and cut new keys for customers. Passersby were often treated to the sight of Mazey Blu, a pet collie, resting in the window.

PJ's Used Records, at 617 Packard Street, weathered CDs, MP3s and streaming music, carrying a large and diverse selection of vinyl LPs. Opened in 1981 by brothers Marc and Jeff Taras, the shop closed in the summer of 2018 after losing its month-to-month lease. A music equipment retailer based in Chicago bought PJ's inventory of sixty thousand records and CDs.

Fingerle Lumber announced that it would be closing in 2019 after eighty-eight years in business. The family-owned business supported numerous local charities and groups and specialized in personalized service not always found in big-box stores.

Independent bookstore Common Language opened in 1991 on Fourth Avenue. Original owners Kate Burkhardt and Lynden Kelly sold the gay and lesbian bookstore to Keith Orr and Martin Contreras in 2003. They moved the shop to Braun Court, an area with a history of LGBTQ activism. While at this location, Common Language expanded its feminist offerings while continuing to offer works by LGBTQ authors. Shop dog Duke, along with owners Orr and Contreras, greeted countless people who were in need of the printed word. They were tireless supporters of local authors, hosting many events and book launches, including one for Images of America: *Downtown Ann Arbor* by coauthor Patti Smith. Their influence on local culture cannot be overstated, and their little corner of Braun Court will be much missed.

ABOUT THE AUTHORS

Current special education teacher and former legal aid lawyer Patti F. Smith is the author of three other books: Images of America: *Downtown Ann Arbor*, *Head Over Feet in Love* and *A History of the People's Food Co-Op Ann Arbor*. She has written for CraftBeer.com, *West Suburban Living* magazine, *Concentrate*, *Mittenbrew*, the *Ann*, AADL's Pulp blog and the *Ann Arbor Observer*. Patti is a frequent public speaker around town, curating *HERsay* (an all-woman variety show) and GROWN FOLKS READING (story time for grownups) and telling stories at Ignite, Nerd Nite, Tellabration and Telling Tales out of School. Patti serves as a commissioner for Recreation Advisory Commission and the county historical commission and as a storyteller in the Ann Arbor Storytellers' Guild, and she volunteers for the Ann Arbor Film Festival and as a DJ for WCBN. Patti leads sold-out local history tours for Rec & Ed, Tammy's Tastings (beer history tours) and By the Sidewalk (food tours). She lives in Ann Arbor with her husband and dog. She can be found online at www.teacherpatti.com.

Britain Woodman works in technology and writes a2retail.space, a photo blog that, despite his best efforts, has become a leading source for retail and commerce news in Ann Arbor. This is his first book published under his real name. Ideally, he would be out visiting every city's beloved, vanishing places, but working on this was cool too.

Visit us at
www.historypress.com